Always Betty

One Woman's Romp Through Life with Grit, Wit, and Wisdom

Always Betty

One Woman's Romp Through Life with
Grit, Wit, and Wisdom

Betty Payte

Always Betty: One Woman's Romp Through Life with Grit, Wit, and Wisdom
Published by Golden Way Publishing
Golden, CO

ISBN: 9781702620796
Personal Memoir
Photos are from the author's private collection

GOLDEN WAY
—PUBLISHING—

To Harold,
you're still the best guy
on the playground.

1941

Dear Ten-Year-Old Betty,

I just ran across a photo of you and your girlfriends when you are in fifth grade. You are standing in the schoolyard in Selby, South Dakota. You have a look of sadness and hopelessness and something else too. Stubbornness? Determination? I remember you feeling unable to do anything right or to please the people you wanted to please—that awful feeling of always being the outsider—never quite belonging.

Let me introduce myself; I am your eighty-eight-year-old self. Seeing that look in your eyes made me want to reach out and tell you that you're going to be okay. You will go on to live a long, productive, and happy life.

You will find that over the years, many people will see more in you than you see in yourself. You may have this feeling of being inadequate, but you will achieve positions of esteem that will surprise you. (They still surprise me!)

Betty, you will find that the curiosity that gets you into trouble will drive you throughout your life and take you to places to do things you can't even imagine at your tender age of ten in 1941. That curiosity comes with a willingness to take chances, to say, "Why not give it a try?"

You will discover your strong inner compass—a sense of right and wrong, an understanding that whatever your dreams, they are achievable. And yes, they involve hard work and lots of give-and-take with others.

So stay curious. Let your curiosity guide you. SPOILER ALERT: You will follow your heroine, Amelia Earhart, and take to the skies yourself—in your own plane. You will learn to scuba dive (after first learning to swim), and ride a bicycle across Austria, and take on jobs that didn't exist in 1941! You will always be looking ahead, seeking just what else is out there. Through the years, that sadness in your eyes will start to lessen. You will blossom into a smart, confident leader who wins awards. Yes, there will be hurdles to get over and challenges to confront, but you have within you the strength and capabilities to meet them and come out stronger for it. Never doubt this: you are meant to be here.

So Betty, go on. Head into the world with those eyes wide open, head held high, standing tall, trusting yourself. Embrace the silly, the tough, and the annoying. And remember to have fun. Don't take things too seriously. What amazing times we live in!

You will shine!

I know. I am you.

Love,

Eighty-Eight-Year-Old Betty

CHAPTER 1

TEXAS

I was born in Texas in 1931, a difficult child in a difficult time and place. They named me Bertha, but I was always Betty right from the start. The Great Depression was coming into full flower, and the Dust Bowl was already raging on the Great Plains. My parents, William and Winnifred Klein, followed the fading promise of work from

Betty on the beach in Galveston, 1933

Dallas to Galveston, where my little brother Billy was born in 1933—but no work.

Desperate, they bundled us and their meager belongings into their raggedy car and headed north to Mobridge, South Dakota, where my Grandpa Klein lived. He was a pretty big deal in Mobridge. As a land agent for the railroad at the turn of the century, he had been assigned the task of plotting out the new town of

One-year-old Betty

Mobridge, where the Milwaukee Railroad Company decided to build the first bridge across the Missouri River (MO+bridge. Get it?) He decided to stay and open his own combined hardware, general, and secondhand store.

On our drive from Texas up to Mobridge, we stopped in South Dakota's Black Hills, where they were only in their seventh year of carving out Mount Rushmore. I remember as a wee three-year-old that it was so darn loud with all that dynamite blowing out the granite mountainside, but luckily Daddy had the great insight to take one of his rare photos of the structure with his squeeze-in, squeeze-out Kodak. In 1933, George Washington was looking good in the rock, and we could even see a hint of Jefferson's eyes and nose, (although later, due to weak stone, they had to move Jefferson) but Roosevelt and Lincoln weren't carved out yet. To this day, it is very meaningful and powerful when we visit the memorial. Just wonder how much effect that wonder had on a three-year-old. (In recent years, I've often joked that I'm older than Mount Rushmore.)

By the time we arrived, Grandma was gone and the Depression had drained off most of Grandpa's wealth and promise. He was not in a good mood. Nor was my Florida-born mother, sentenced to live in that cold, dusty, dead-end prairie town surrounded by unwelcoming in-laws. So it wasn't long before

Mount Rushmore, October 1933

she, in a small act of rebellion, bought the more expensive coffee instead of the cheapest. Grandpa objected to her wasteful ways, and we soon moved to a small two-bedroom rented house on the edge of town.

Grandpa had secured a job for Dad in the Red Owl Grocery Store, where you could buy pickled herring by the pound from an open barrel. It was right next door to the hardware and general store Grandpa started when times had been flush. Mobridge was situated next door to the Standing Rock Indian Reservation, and the elderly Sioux men would gather on the sidewalk outside. I had to summon all of my courage and walk very, very fast to get past them to the door. They never threatened me, of course. Later, I grew to love the drums and dancing during the powwows they held on the reservation. Both my father and grandfather spoke Sioux fluently and did a lot of business with the tribe.

Our life settled into the quiet pattern of small-town living. We walked everywhere—from the store for kerosene for the stove to the park where the homegrown city band played concerts on summer evenings and my father played the cornet. Later, we walked the several blocks to school.

We attended the Episcopal Church just around the corner from our house, where on Palm Sunday, we carried palm fronds tied into crosses, and on Christmas, the boys borrowed their father's bathrobes to wear as costumes to play shepherds for the annual Christmas program.

On June 4, 1936, we got a new baby sister, Nancy Lee. My most vivid memory of baby Nancy was the day my mother had left her sleeping in her basket weave carriage. I tried to climb up to see if she was really sleeping and tipped her over into a snowbank. Boy, did I catch it! I was sentenced to stay in my bedroom for the rest of the day. As I remember it, I screamed and hollered all day.

Meanwhile, Billy, then three, was also branching out—way out. He developed a habit of running away. One day, my mother got an idea. She ran a rope through the straps of his overalls and hitched him up to the clothesline, so he could run the length of clothesline, safely secured. But Billy was clever. She went out later and found Billy gone and his overalls on the ground—he'd simply unbuckled them and wiggled free.

We had the usual family inconveniences. When I was about five, I came down with scarlet fever and was put on bedrest for what seemed like weeks. In fact, the whole house was quarantined, so no one could come in or go out. My father brought food and passed it through the kitchen window. I spent my time cutting out paper dolls. When I finally recovered, we had to burn them all.

Less serious, but scary for me, was the day I was riding with Aunt Mary and Uncle John, when a tire on the car blew out just as we were crossing a bridge and the car tipped over. Luckily, I was sitting on Aunt Mary's lap and she held on tightly. Otherwise, I might have been thrown out of the car and into the river. I didn't want to even ride in a car for a long time after that.

There were scarier times, too, of course. My Aunt Mary lived in our town and was definitely part of our extended family. I sometimes stayed overnight with them. She was diagnosed with breast cancer, and we watched as she grew weaker and sicker. I remember her last days were spent in her bedroom surrounded by candles—very scary for a five-year-old.

We also lost two cousins tragically. Jackie died in a fishing accident when his boat turned over and his high fishing boots filled with water. He couldn't get out of them, and he drowned. Junior died while demonstrating his flying skills with his brand-new airplane. It went into a dive, and he crashed while well-wishers watched in horror.

CHAPTER 2

SELBY, SOUTH DAKOTA

When I was seven, my dad was elected county auditor for Walworth County, and we moved to Selby, the county seat, about twenty-two miles from Mobridge. We moved into a big yellow house, a two-story duplex; the landlord lived upstairs, and we had the first floor. We arrived in Selby just in time for me to start second grade. I was not impressed. The school was pretty nondescript, which really didn't matter since (in my memory) it was hidden by snow from October to May.

There were two grades in each classroom, but beyond that, I don't remember much. I do remember the ugly brown stockings all the girls wore through the cold weather months. Girls were required to wear dresses in those days, hence the need for leg coverings—and hence garter belts that invariably pulled and pinched throughout the day and revealed themselves in unexpected and embarrassing ways. I longed for the first warm days of spring when I could wear anklets again. I hated those stockings.

In warmer weather, the boys spent recess playing competitive games of marbles; the girls mostly played jacks or hopscotch. Sometimes, it was jumping rope, jumping in rhythm as the spectators chanted:

> Cinderella dressed in yella,
> Went downstairs to kiss her fella;
> How many kisses did she give him?
> One … two … three …

as they counted out the jumps. Or maybe:

> Teddy bear, teddy bear turn around,
> Teddy bear, teddy bear, touch the ground.

as jumpers turned and touched. Also:

> Mabel, Mabel set the table …
> And don't forget …
> … the red hot peppers …

at which point, the rope speeded up until the jumper gave in.

At home, decades before television came to the plains, we kids would gather by the small dome-shaped Zenith radio and listen to our favorite programs: *Little Orphan Annie*, *Captain Midnight*, *The Lone Ranger*, and *Jack Armstrong, the All-American Boy*. I ordered a cardboard cockpit from Captain Midnight, which I planted in a strategic spot where I would listen and pretend I was flying the plane. It was the beginning of my lifelong love affair with flying.

Billy and I got a new sled for Christmas one year, and we headed almost immediately for what was generously called Ski Jump Hill, which featured a high lip that could, under the right conditions, send a sled flying. Conditions were perfect, and our new sled, on its first run, landed with a thump and broke into several pieces. We bawled all the way home.

Class systems reveal themselves even in the tiniest of communities. The Michelsons had the biggest, fanciest house in town and apparently other attributes that made them special, since one of them went on to become the governor of South Dakota. Greta Schmitt, daughter of the town butcher, had the very nicest clothes of anyone in our class and a walk-in playhouse. Jealousy, I guess, overcame any good sense, and my girlfriends and I found a way to throw Greta's precious playhouse into a complete mess. One more time in trouble, and we probably learned nothing from it.

Some of our ideas were more—shall we say—well-meaning. Since we both loved reading and the whole atmosphere of the library, my friend Sarah Moos and I decided to build a library of our own in the haymow of her family's barn as a summer project. Of course, the result never came close to the grand library we had envisioned, but the dream itself kept us busy and out of trouble for a good part of the summer.

Billy and I were always on the lookout for ways to make money. At the tender age of five, I stole three pennies from the kitchen counter of a neighbor who was operating a small kindergarten for us. My mother was horrified when she discovered what I'd done and marched me back to the teacher to admit my guilt and accept any punishment. I vowed to change my ways. But I soon discovered other ways besides thievery to get into trouble.

As we got bigger our opportunities for employment expanded. At eight, I offered to watch the neighbor's little boy who was disinclined to listen to me and promptly toddled his way into the street. I earned no payment or a good referral for that one.

Later, Billy and I worked together to pick up milk from a nearby farmer and deliver it to his customers in town. Too soon, we grew bored with the everlasting sameness of it all. We started singing along the route. This was a favorite:

Sweetly sings the donkey as he goes to hay,
Kee I Kee O, Kee I Kee O Kee A,
Someone must go with him, or he'll run away.
Kee I Kee O, Kee I Kee O Kee A.

We sang as loudly as we could, probably hoping to get fired. If so, it didn't work. Finally one day, we just hid everyone's milk behind the barn and went home. That was the end of that job.

My next job was at the local hairdresser, using a magnet to pick up bobby pins from the floor. I don't remember how that one ended. I think there just weren't enough dropped bobby pins to keep me on.

In May 1942, at the end of my fifth-grade year, the war had begun. My dad's term as auditor was also over and he took a job with the government on Attu Island in Alaska. The rest of us—Mother, me, Billy, and Nancy—moved to Wheat Ridge, Colorado, to be near her sister, Aunt Bertha, and Uncle Lyle.

Best of all, in more enlightened Colorado, girls were allowed to wear anklets all year. In cold weather, ski pants were encouraged. I was officially freed from the dreaded brown stockings.

Chapter 3

Colorado

The bus ride to Colorado from South Dakota felt long, but to us it was a grand adventure. We hardly ever went anywhere since we had no car, and we only got out of town if someone offered to drive us. We stopped halfway (I think it was in Custer), and for the first time ever, we stayed in a hotel. We marveled at the big white water pitcher and bowl.

Housing was scarce in Colorado, and housing we could afford was even harder to find. My Aunt Bertha found a small garage not too far from where she lived. It had no inside plumbing and no bathroom, and our access to water was a small pump in the kitchen sink. This would be our first experience using an outhouse, and it was NOT fun. It was right out in back of the garage, but in the cold winter months you wondered if it might be better to suffer with crossed legs all night rather than get bundled up

Klein family photo in front of their garage house, circa 1944
Left to right: Billy, Betty, Mother, Nancy

and wander into the snow in the dark and feel your way around the wood shed. Mother kept a white chamber pot under the bed to use for nighttime emergencies.

There were two small rooms. One had a bed at one end—that was Mother's—and a couch at the other end next to the garage door that Nancy and I pulled out every night to sleep on. Billy slept in the tiny, stuffy attic space, which he entered by way of a rope ladder. A kitchen stove, a small sink with a pump, and a little round table filled the other room. We took our baths in the same galvanized tub Mother used for rinsing laundry with water we carried from the kitchen pump and heated on the stove. We had baths once a week and all shared the water.

Our front yard was a small apple orchard, and we took full advantage of that by climbing the trees and eating the apples.

The war effort was gearing up, and Mother found a job at the nearby Remington Arms Munition Plant. My dad had gone to

Attu, and the three of us started school at Fruitdale Elementary, about a mile from our house. I was in sixth grade, Billy in fourth, and Nancy started first grade.

Mother left early and worked late, and that left the three of us to get ourselves to school. After school, we were alone until the evening, when Mother came home. As the oldest (I was eleven), I was in charge of seeing that the other two got ready and got to school on time. They definitely didn't want to take orders from me. And yes, I was sometimes bossy and impatient. One time, a teacher called me out of the classroom and said Nancy was not clean enough and that I should do something about it. I have forgotten what, if anything, I did.

We all had impetigo outbreaks from time to time. Apparently, that is quite contagious and required some kind of a purple medicinal salve all over our faces. Contagious, purple-faced kids were not allowed to come to school—another hurdle.

Nancy reported that one of her classmates told her that her mother bathed her every night and rubbed her with lotion. Nancy thought they must be very rich to have a life like that. She thought that having her own room would be the closest thing to heaven she could imagine.

Every morning the whole school would gather in the front yard, face the flag, and repeat the Pledge of Allegiance. Then we sang the state song:

Just got back to my mile-high shack,
In that wonderful, wonderful, wonderful state of mine,
With its stop, look, listen, not a hilltop missin',
And the sun just likes to shine.

So its C O L O hip hip R A D O,
Tell the world I'm feeling fine.

My teacher seemed to take a special interest in me. She helped me get elected president of the Jefferson County Colorado Young Citizens League (CYCL). She never seemed to understand that I was petrified and had to hold my knees together at the front table to keep them from knocking. She also had me lead a group of students in front of the Mothers' Club, reciting and explaining the poem "Ode to a Waterfowl."

There was one boy in the sixth grade I thought was different from the rest. He didn't tease and chase the girls around like the other boys. How civilized! How grown-up! At recess one day, when we were playing ball, I scooped up a ball hit to center field and threw it to the catcher.

As we headed back to the classroom, he said, "Boy, you sure don't throw like a girl!"

So I said, "I throw like my dad taught me."

Later, I heard him tell someone that I could throw the ball further than any other girl in the sixth grade and if the ball was hit into the outfield, I was the only one who could be counted on to throw it home in time. His name was Harold Payte.

Harold and I started talking a lot. I liked him—I mean, for a boy. His family moved to Oregon for a while, then returned to Colorado, and we jumped back into our friendship. Then they moved to Arkansas. The couple of years he was in Arkansas, he wrote me some letters, which impressed me to no end. I was definitely happy when they moved back to Colorado for good.

When we were in eighth grade, I was in the local 4H club.
The club sponsored a roller-skating party, and we were supposed
to ask someone to go with us. I asked Harold and was surprised
when he said yes. Our only mode of transportation was the old
interurban (streetcar) line that ran about a mile from our house.
The plan was that he would come by my house to get me and
together we would walk to our stop.

It turned out to be a rainy night, and when our agreed-upon
time arrived, he didn't show up. I assumed he decided not to go,
so I walked on to the streetcar by myself. When he did get to my
house, Mother told him I had gone on, so he ran and got there
just in time for the arrival of the streetcar. He explained that he
had ducked under a large billboard to get out of the rain, which
caused his delay. We had a great evening skating with all of our
friends, and on the ride home he reached over and took my hand.
He held it all the way home. That was our first, sort of, date.

CHAPTER 4

TEEN YEARS

World War II was in full gear as I entered my teen years. Gabriel Heater's nightly radio broadcast usually opened with the statement, "There's bad news tonight." Occasionally we heard, "There is good news tonight." We hung on his every word.

The war had a profound effect on me. We could watch the tracer bullets, little lighted tracks in the sky when they were testing the ammunition that came from the plant where Mother worked. We were near Lowry Field, and we would try to identify the planes that flew over. It got to the point where we could easily recognize the P38—they had twin tails with a space between them—and the big bomber planes, the B52s and B29s. When the newspapers came out with pictures and maps of how the Allies were being forced into retreat, it seemed as if we were about to be invaded at any time.

Of course, I understood that we were a very long way from the fighting, but I often had an irrational fear that the Germans (or the Italians or the Japanese) were ready to breach the Nebraska border. I remembered back in South Dakota, there were a couple of German families that people looked down on and sometimes treated badly, and that was before the war had even started.

One year, I won a small silver ring at our school's Spring Field Day, and I had to get up onstage in the auditorium and announce what I had wished for on that ring. I had wished for the war to be over and the boys to come back home. The way I said it made the audience think I was mainly interested in having boys back, and they laughed at me. I was so embarrassed.

I really did HATE the war and all it stood for. We had to deal with ration stamps and were somewhat limited in what we could buy, so we did experience some of the marginal consequences of the war. I do remember the ration books and a lot of peanut butter sandwiches, yet we always had enough to eat.

Because Wheat Ridge was a farming community, my friends and I could get jobs right away in the summertime. At first we weeded carrots, then picked strawberries and raspberries when they were ready, and picked corn and threw it into tall horse-drawn wagons. This was not a very pleasant job, as the leaves of the corn plant were sharp and slashed us as we went by.

When a crop peaked, it needed to be picked immediately, and the farmers hired anybody they could—even the boys from the nearby reform school. One farmer, a Swedish lady, was pretty unhappy with the help they sent from the school. She said they smashed the berries so badly they couldn't be used for anything but "yams and yellies." We thought that was very funny. I really loved the idea of being able to work and earn some money on my own.

When we were a little older, we went to work in the celery fields. The Fruitdale Valley was known for its superior Colorado Pascal celery. When it was full-grown, it was wrapped into folded newspapers and left standing in the fields. The function of the wrapping was to keep the sun away from the stalk and to bleach it. It also kept the wind from blowing it around and developing tough fibers. This practice made it uniquely crisp and tender. Any celery left standing at the time of possible frost was cut and kicked into trenches twelve inches wide by twelve inches deep and then covered with newspaper and straw. Around Thanksgiving, the trenches were opened, and the celery that came out of the ground was quite white and free of the normal strings that celery has.

Our eighth-grade graduation class consisted of twelve students: six boys and six girls. I was valedictorian. What was memorable about the graduation was the speaker—but not because his speech was so inspiring. His hairpiece moved around his head as he spoke and wafted in the breeze if he paused. I don't remember anything he had to say. But I *do* remember his hair.

Fruitdale School only went to eighth grade, so after graduation, we had a choice of going to Golden, Wheat Ridge, or Arvada High School. I decided on Wheat Ridge, where my cousin was going. Not that Peggy and I had such a great relationship, but Aunt Bertha could drive us to school.

Wheat Ridge High School was a huge change—going from a twelve-student class at Fruitdale to a class of over 100 students in the freshman class at Wheat Ridge. These kids had all been to a junior high school together and seemed to know each other. I didn't know any of them, and I had a hard time fitting in. School was never very fun for me. I had no close friends and lived so far away, I couldn't participate in any after-school activities.

Between my eighth and ninth grade years, my mother purchased a small house on Independence Lane near 44th Avenue. It was larger than the garage house, but it still had no bathroom or inside running water. Another small kitchen sink with a pump furnished water for the house.

This time, however, there was a long room in the attic. Nancy and I had a bed at one end, and Billy had a narrow bed in the hall that led to that room. My mother didn't have a real bedroom, either, just a small bed under the stairs leading to the attic.

The house sat on an acre and a half of land, part of which was sown in alfalfa; later on, she planted a large garden. Asparagus grew wild on the ditch bank. Mother canned a lot of the vegetables she grew. Canning the pickled beets was always a very messy job, but well worth the effort. The beets tasted wonderful. She also grew gladiolas, which she took out to the Veterans Hospital when they had reached full bloom. She always took great pride in being able to share their flowers.

After three years, my father returned from Attu in the summer of 1945, shortly after we moved. He had always been moody and impatient with us—especially me—so it took some getting used to having him around again. He brought me a coat from Alaska that had a large hood with fur trim. It never seemed quite like the right thing to wear, but I liked it. After he got home, he bought a 1940 green Nash, our first car since we moved from Texas to South Dakota in 1933. My mother didn't learn to drive until she was in her mid-forties.

The news came over the radio that the war had ended and our whole family jumped on the streetcar to head into Downtown Denver to join in the celebration. The soldiers filled the streets, kissing all the girls. My dad was furious when one of them came after me as I was trying to back up and get away from him.

With Dad home, he found a job working for the American Standard Plumbing Supply, where he worked until he retired. My mother worked at Shaeffer Tent and Awning Company after her job at the Remington Arms Plant came to an end.

Billy started a paper route delivering the *Denver Post*. His route covered several miles, a long way to ride a bicycle, especially carrying papers. Later, he bought a small horse named Dixie, which he rode to deliver papers. He had trained Dixie to stop at Bill's Tavern. She would stand with her front legs on the cement step at the back door and wait for someone to bring her some bread. Occasionally, I had to take over the route for Billy and had to ride the horse; I could not get her to go by the tavern without stopping, something I did not want her to do.

At the end of the month, collecting for the paper was an ordeal for everyone. Billy loved delivering the papers and talking to everyone on the route, but he did not like to collect for the subscriptions. Every month it was the same thing—Billy wouldn't collect and Daddy would yell and bat him around awhile. It never changed.

Betty at 16

CHAPTER 5

BECOMING ADULTS

Harold and I started to see each other more. Our dates were mostly movies, ball games, hiking at Red Rocks, and fishing with our friends Bob Seger and Ida Mae Harrell. While Harold's brother, Roy, was away at college, we had access to his car, a green 1931 Chrysler.

We were thrilled to have a car, but there were many times we had to push it to get it started when the battery ran down. The roof leaked, so when it rained, we had to hold something over our heads to keep dry. And the floorboards were not tight, so when there was rain or snow on the ground, the water would splash up through them, and we had to lift our legs so we wouldn't get wet. Still, it took us to the ball games of the Wheat Ridge Farmers and occasionally a movie at the theater in Arvada on a Saturday night. We paid sixty cents for the tickets. One time we were at a ball game in Arvada, and as Harold was turning around in someone's driveway, the battery dropped out of the car. The boys took off their belts to temporarily hang the battery in place until we got home. It worked!

Harold drove Roy's old 1931 Chrysler until he bought the 1936 Plymouth we drove for years. It showed up with a for sale sign on it at a filling station about two blocks from the Saline Feed, the Purina feed dealership where he worked.

None of my classes interested me much at Wheat Ridge High; some, like algebra, were just difficult. Latin was kind of fun, and I actually have used it to figure out words and their meanings.

Gym class was led by an English teacher who really didn't know and didn't seem to care very much about what we were doing. The funniest thing I remember was one of my classmates, Lizzy, standing and waving her arms in front of me as I tried to shoot a basket in our half-a-gym-floor basketball game. I couldn't stop laughing long enough to finish the job.

I sang in the musical programs at Christmas and was a member of Pep Club in my junior year. We wore little blue skirts with jackets that had a Farmer, the school mascot, emblem on it. Blue-and-white saddle shoes completed our outfits. It was our job to cheer on the boys' teams during their games.

We were supposed to wear these shoes only at ball games, but I didn't think I should ask my parents for another pair of shoes just for Pep Club, so I wore them as my everyday shoes. The president of the Pep Club asked me about them. I lied and said I had two pairs. I don't think they believed me, but they didn't press the matter.

Harold was getting more bored and impatient with school. He couldn't see that it was preparing him in any way for the future and felt he was only wasting his time.

"What does knowing the date of the Treaty of Ghent have to do with anything?" he asked.

He wanted to start earning money. He already had a pretty good part-time job at the Climie's turkey farm. One day, he told me their Purina feed dealer needed help because two drivers were off sick. Harry Willis, the owner, hired Harold to fill in for one day.

Then he said, "Come back Monday; we'll find something for you to do."

The pay was thirty-five dollars a week, and the hours were 7:00 a.m. to 6:00 p.m., six days a week. He quit school in the middle of the eleventh grade to work for Purina fulltime.

Colorado high schools at that time required sixteen credits to graduate, and I had fifteen. I needed only one more year of English literature to graduate. Yet, I eventually quit school too.

Harold and I started to talk seriously about getting married by the end of my junior year, the spring of 1948. Harold had a steady job he liked, and I was more than ready to leave an unhappy home life, as Daddy was growing more and more intolerable. I didn't really have any plans for after high school that didn't include Harold. And, of course, we knew we were deeply in love. We were seventeen and eighteen, so we pretty much knew everything there was to know.

There was no formal marriage proposal. That's just not how things were done in 1948. But rather, the idea evolved. And once the decision was made, the first hurdle was telling my parents. We needed their permission since I was only seventeen. Picking me up for our dates had always been an obstacle course for Harold. He first had to get by Toby, the big, black Chow dog who was chained to the back step and growled whenever Harold tried to get to the door. Toby always scared him. Then he had to come inside to face my dad, who sat in his big easy chair with the *Denver Post* up in front of his nose. He would lower his paper just enough so Harold could see his glasses; then he would glower at Harold, utter a guttural "grumph," and pull the paper back up over his face.

Telling my parents we wanted to get married felt like that gauntlet—times ten. I finally dodged the whole thing. I told my mother, who told my father, who said if I ran off and got married, "You make that bed and you'll have to sleep in it. Don't think you can ever come home to stay again!"

I was never even tempted to return.

CHAPTER 6

EARLY MARRIED LIFE

The wedding was on a Saturday evening, September 4, 1948, at the home of the justice of the peace in Golden, Colorado. My parents, Harold's parents, our friends Bob and Ida Mae, the justice of the peace and his wife, and Harold and I were the only people there. I wore the dark green dress I'd found at J.C. Penney in Downtown Denver. Harold bought a grey suit that became what he wore to weddings and funerals well into the '70s. We went to sign the official license before the wedding and discovered in the space for "bride's name" that the clerk at the courthouse had written Ida Mae Harrell's name instead of mine. That caused some good-natured teasing and a little anxiety that "now Harold had to marry Ida Mae." Thankfully, in the end, the justice of the peace just scratched her name off and put in mine. All was well. That small faux pas became a lifelong joke, as Harold often introduced me as his second wife.

Harold had never been to a wedding before, so every time the justice of the peace paused, Harold said, "I do!" And, with that, we started our journey together.

After the wedding, both sets of parents went home, and the four of us went to Cottage Hill Drive Inn for hamburgers and malts—exactly what we would have done on any other Saturday night.

Harold and Betty on their wedding day, September 4, 1948

Harold had rented a very small house that belonged to a neighbor of his parents for twenty-five dollars a month. Some of my girlfriends pooled their money and bought us a set of dishes. It was our only wedding present.

The next morning, our good friend Leon Haile came to our door with food to cook for our breakfast. What a happy surprise, especially since he had to wade through an overflowing irrigation ditch to get to our little abode. We invited him to stay and eat with us, but he said no.

We were not even settled into this tiny place when we came home one rainy day to find the roof leaking and the bed soaking wet. We lived there for less than a month. Within a couple of days, we found a remodeled one-room chicken coop a couple of miles east of where we were. There was still no indoor plumbing, but the rent was a little less—twenty-five dollars for the leaky place and twenty-two for the chicken coop. On Harold's pay of thirty-five dollars a week, we saved some money—enough for a date of hamburgers, malts, and a movie every Saturday night.

The following May, eight months after our September wedding, we took a delayed honeymoon and drove our 1936 Plymouth to Texas City, Texas, where we visited my Aunt Vera and Uncle Earl, then on to Arkansas, where we visited some of Harold's relatives and friends, and completed our trip in Missouri, visiting Harold's older sister, Hazle, and her family.

We started our trip with $105 and came home with $40. Mostly, we stayed with friends and relatives and slept in the car if they weren't nearby. We stopped at little stores for bread and bologna when we needed something to eat—not exactly a deluxe honeymoon, but we were as happy as a pair of puppies.

In Arkansas, we visited the place where Harold's family lived in Potter. It was at a junction of two gravel roads with a store on each side of the railroad track. It was about seven miles south of the larger town of Mena. Harold said the house and the hanging footbridge were gone from the old home place, but other than that, not much had changed from when he lived there several years before. At one place, the bridge was out, and we had to drive through the creek. When the water came up to the bottom of the doors, I had a small panic, but we made it.

In Salem, Missouri, we stayed a few days with Harold's sister and brother-in-law, Hazle and Bill Dunning, and their four children. Bill took us squirrel and rabbit hunting. I found a rabbit just sitting there in my sights, and I couldn't pull the trigger. That was pretty much the beginning and end of my hunting career. One morning, we came out to breakfast and found our cereal bowls overflowing with Wheaties. Their kids wanted the masks that were on the back of the cereal boxes, and they saw us as an opportunity to help empty them.

From there, it was straight back to Wheat Ridge. Our trip fit neatly into a two-week vacation.

Flora McCarty was our landlady while we lived in our little chicken house. She and I spent a lot of time together. She taught me how to crochet, to cook a little, and how to chop the heads off of chickens. There was a tree stump in the yard with two nails placed just wide enough apart to stretch the chicken's neck so we could chop the heads off with an ax. I really hated doing that. We didn't have chicken dinners very often.

We lived in that house until our first child, Patty, was born on February 26, 1950. Henry gave Harold a raise of two dollars and fifty cents, which brought his wages up to thirty-seven fifty a week. We saved money on that, as we only had to fill the gas tank once a week.

The Plymouth wouldn't start when the weather was cold, so Harold would hitch a ride to work. Then Flora and I would start it after the day warmed up and drive it around to charge the battery. Neither one of us had driver's licenses, so we used the time to practice our driving skills. When we thought we were proficient enough, we drove to Golden and both got our driver's licenses.

While I was in the hospital giving birth to Patty, Harold brought both grandmothers out to see the new baby. They had to get down on their knees to see under the bottom of the shade that covered the window of the hospital nursery. But they didn't seem to mind—the two grandmothers oohed and aahed about how beautiful she was. In the fifties, it was standard for mothers to spend five days in the hospital after delivering a baby, and we were expected to stay in bed all that time.

After Patty was born, we moved to 8100 North Pecos in Westminster. It was a small rental house on Harold's boss's farm—with inside plumbing! For the first time in our adult lives, we didn't have to walk outside to use a bathroom.

Within a few days of the move, I started hemorrhaging. It was so bad we had to call the doctor and his wife, who was also the nurse, out in the middle of the night. They ordered me to stay in bed for a few days as the best way to treat it. My sister Nancy and Harold's sister Nelline came out to the farm to help with the new baby. The doctors discovered that I was Rh negative. Apparently, being Rh negative means you don't have a certain protein on the surface of your red blood cells. There's normally no problem, unless you're pregnant. If your blood and your baby's blood mix, your body will start to wreak all kinds of havoc. Harold was tested, too, and discovered that he was also Rh negative—a rare happening.

I thought this all meant that we would probably not be able to have more children. Because I'd had such a rough time, I was tempted not to tell anyone and to let everyone think we were not supposed to have any more children. I thought about it a long time but finally did confess the truth about the Rh negative results. It turned out I misunderstood the Rh factor. We would be able to have more children after all. If Harold had been Rh *positive*, that would have been the problem.

Life on the farm was very lonely for me. We had no close neighbors, and Harold worked from seven in the morning until six at night, six days a week. I knew nothing about babies and had no way to learn about mothering. So I just made sure to give baby Patty a daily bath, fed her when she was hungry, and changed her when she was wet. That seemed to take care of it. When she was a very tiny baby, I would wheel her down the road in a doll carriage to meet Harold on his way home from work.

When Patty was about three, she wandered away from the fenced yard, and I found her across the street, walking among a herd of Black Angus cattle. It really frightened me that she could get away so quickly, and I was so relieved when I found her.

CHAPTER 7

BUILDING A FUTURE

In 1952, while we were living on the farm on North Pecos, we purchased a lot from the Climies, who were dividing up their turkey farm in Wheat Ridge. The lot was 100 feet by 190 feet, and we paid $750 for it. That was a lot of money at that time, and Mrs. Climie's sister carried the papers. When we were about to get it paid off, I had a dream that we went to them with the final payment. They said they didn't know what we were talking about and had never seen us before. It was only a dream, but I remained nervous until the final papers were signed.

Our plan was to build a large garage toward the back of the property with the intention of building a house with a breezeway later. Our friend Bob Seger, a builder, helped us lay out the foundation. We purchased cinder blocks for the building as we could afford them and then spent most of our Sundays laying blocks for the walls. We had a well drilled and built a little pump house for the pump so we would have water to mix mortar and cement. Then vandals pushed over one wall, and it took us nearly six weeks to reconstruct it.

After we had repaired the damage, we decided to stay in the comfortable house on North Pecos and rent out the garage instead. We eventually sold it to people who, it turned out, couldn't keep up their payments. We decided we had to foreclose on them. But they just left, probably in the middle of the night. Before they left, though, they took the pump, dropped the pipe into the well, and generally trashed the place. That meant a new well had to be drilled. We couldn't afford the price of cleanup and a new well, so we sold it as is, just about holding our investment together.

We raised a Yorkshire sow from a weaning pig. When she got older, we sold her piglets as weanlings. We raised broiler (frying) chickens and a calf for meat. Our black cocker spaniel dog, Shadow, had a litter of pups. So we had quite a menagerie.

One evening, as Harold was cleaning the calf's pen, the calf got out, ran down the driveway to the road, and took off. Harold ran after the calf, and the dog with her puppies and the little piglets ran after Harold. What a sight! It looked like a Disney cartoon.

To feed this menagerie, Harold brought feed home every night. When payday came around, the feed bill was deducted from his salary. One week, he brought home a dollar and a half—the next week, three dollars. There was essentially no food in the house. I found a potato and one egg and made potato salad. We decided I should go to work.

I started working at Montgomery Ward in the catalog department, packing and shipping orders to be mailed. This meant I had to take Harold to work in North Denver before 7:00 a.m., then Patty to either my mother's in Wheat Ridge or one of Harold's nieces in Arvada. Then I would drive myself to work on South Broadway in Denver. At five, I would reverse the procedure and arrive home after seven at night. Harold would take care of the animals while I fixed dinner. This was our routine for a couple of years.

No surprise then that through all this we didn't have any social life with friends, just occasional get-togethers with family. The people I met at Wards were work-only friends, but we did a lot of chatting during our lunchtimes. I welcomed this change, as I had no one to talk with on the farm.

We moved to Wheat Ridge when Patty was about three, into another farmhouse that was owned by Harold's boss. It was near 38th and Wadsworth. There, we had an alfalfa field, about 100 laying hens, and a field of sweet corn. We put a sign on the street and sold eggs and sweet corn at the door. People were very honest—if we weren't available, they left the money on the back porch for whatever they bought.

When we moved from North Pecos, we brought along our dog, a little brown-and-white mixed breed named Spike. We got a call from the people who moved in after us, telling us that our dog was back at their house. He had navigated twelve to fifteen miles across busy streets and unfamiliar neighborhoods. We picked him up and brought him home, and he disappeared again. We waited for the phone call, but this time, none came. Sometime later, we heard he was living with a family who lived two miles away from us. Since he and the family he'd adopted seemed very happy together, we left him there.

In 1954, we packed up our green 1948 Ford pickup--complete with the camper shell that Harold had built on the back—and took a road trip to Oregon to visit Harold's brother Floyd and his family. When the truck got to a certain speed, the wind whistling through the grill changed tones and let us know we should check our speed. Somewhere in the Utah desert, we set a bag of our shoes under the truck and drove away. An unfortunate mistake!

Our social life improved when we discovered that two families from other Purina dealerships lived nearby. We went dancing several times with Toby and Kay Oliver at Elitch Gardens and Lakeside Amusement Park. Tommy Dorsey's band played at Lakeside. One of our dance venues was a grand ballroom that had a large, sparkling chandelier that spun around and around. Harold's brother Robert played guitar in a Western band at the VFW hall on South Broadway, where we went dancing several times.

Television was just becoming mainstream, and we would take our chips and dip and meet at Bob and Gladys Ipson's home to watch George Gobel. They were the first in our group to get a TV. Saturday nights became pretty special.

Eventually, we were able to buy a television set of our own. *Mickey Mouse Club* and the *Grand Old Opry* were two of our favorite programs. Compared to today, we had very few program choices, and they were all in black and white.

My sister, Nancy, came to live with us for a time when she was finishing high school and before she joined the Marine Corps. It seems she'd also had enough of living at home.

The Purina Dog Chow route became available, and Harold left Saline Feed to run this business. He drove a big blue panel truck that he used to pick up dog food at the warehouse and deliver it to grocery stores, feed stores, and veterinarians. This job came to an end when the large grocery stores like Safeway began getting their dog food through their own warehouses.

Harold went back to Saline Feed, where he ran the lawnmower and small engine repair shop until a manager position opened up at Farmers Feed and Supply Store in Arvada. He was a manager there until 1969. The Willises owned all the stores that Harold worked at over the years.

Our daughter, Amy, was born on August 1, 1955. Henry Willis, Harold's boss, thought we should call her Columbine, the state flower, since August 1 is Colorado Day. I'm glad we decided against that.

Patty started kindergarten at Wilmore Davis Elementary and stayed there through first grade, when we bought our first home on 48th Avenue, just three blocks east of Wadsworth, still in Wheat Ridge. We paid $12,500 for it. The house had been divided into two units. We lived on one side and rented the other. Our mortgage payments were $72.00 a month, and we charged $75.00 for rent for the smaller apartment.

Although life was going well, I remember one day when my mind went to a very dark place. As I was standing in the dining room of our beautiful first home, I had a brief thought of suicide. Out of the blue. I had no idea where it came from. There was no desire to actually do something about it—just a momentary thought that the world would be better off without me.

CHAPTER 8

RAISING A FAMILY

On Amy's first day of kindergarten, she had come home very disappointed. I asked what had happened, and she answered, "You said I would learn to read when I went to school. I was there all day, and I still can't read!"

Even before she went to preschool, she would sit opposite me when I was ironing and we would "read" to each other. So I guess when she finally started school, she thought she would magically know how to read from the first day, just as we had been doing at home. Kids are so literal!

The following year, when Amy was in first grade and Patty was in fifth grade in Martenson School, President Kennedy was killed. Amy was so deeply affected by this that I went to the school nurse to see if there was something I could do to help her through it. She told me that Amy was both very intelligent and

Payte family photo, 1960
Left to right: Betty, Harold, Patty, Amy

highly sensitive, and she seemed to sense the significance of this more than the other first graders. It took a while for her to be able to function normally again. She was afraid to go to bed, afraid to cross the street, afraid to go to school, and afraid not to. She cried a lot.

A couple of years later, we bought the girls a set of World Book Encyclopedias for a Christmas present, and she would say, "If Karen (her friend) comes over, tell her I'm upstairs reading the 'cyclopedia."

Amy continued to be a very interesting little girl to raise. Sometimes it seemed she could almost read my thoughts. Once, when I was driving the car and she was sitting down low on the seat beside me, she said, "Be careful when you drive, Mommy; we don't want to run over any dogs!"

There was a dead dog lying in the gutter right next to where I was turning, and there was no way she could have seen it. Another time, we were at a local bank and the fellow helping us looked like someone I had known in high school, but I wasn't sure. As we were leaving, Amy said, "That man back there was Chuck." She had no way of knowing that, and I surely hadn't discussed it with her. I found out later that he was, indeed, named Chuck.

She wanted to read everything. One day, we were at a car wash when she asked what the word was after "car." I told her the word was "wash." She said no, that couldn't be, because it didn't have an "r" in it. I guess it sounded to her as if we were saying "car warsh," which we probably were.

Both girls continued to grow and expand in their abilities. Eventually, we bought Aunt Bertha's upright piano for ten dollars. It was quite old, but we had it tuned and found it to be a very good piano. Patty started taking piano lessons from Mrs. Brandorff and eventually from her husband, Professor Brandorff. She did well and seemed to enjoy the piano. There was never a problem getting her to practice.

When she was a little older, I started teaching her to sew. Our neighbor wanted her daughter to learn to sew as well, but she didn't know how to sew herself, much less how to teach someone else. So we traded lessons—she taught Patty to knit and I taught her daughter to sew.

Academics were not so easy for Patty, but she worked hard at her classes. Mr. Nocton was her sixth grade teacher. He tried to prepare them for junior high by giving them a lot of writing assignments during the school year. Patty always drew pictures to go along with her stories, and Mr. Nocton would leave comments on them. He thought the pictures were funny. He concluded that she was more of an illustrator than a writer.

With her exposure to sewing, junior high sewing classes were easy for Patty. Their teacher planned a style show for parents and grandparents featuring the clothes they had made in class. When Patty came onstage, my dad broke into VERY loud applause, shouting and whistling. Patty was mortified.

It always bothered me that I never finished high school. How could I impress upon our kids the importance of a good education when I hadn't completed high school myself?

At the time, there wasn't such a thing as a GED that would allow nongraduates to earn a diploma. When I left high school, I needed only sixteen credits, but by then, the number had been raised to twenty credits. The only way to get that diploma was to take the classes I needed to bring my total up to twenty.

I took classes in history (the teacher thought the South had won the Civil War), two sewing classes (where I made myself a suit and learned a lot more about sewing), and some English and literature classes. The teacher called and asked me to see her about the tests in the English classes that I'd taken. She told me I rated so high that I definitely didn't need the classes, but since the system didn't allow for that, I took the classes anyway.

It was very interesting to be in classes with students so much younger than myself (I was about thirty), so when we read short stories, I understood them from quite a different perspective than the sixteen-year-olds. For instance, several of the stories that I found to be tragic, they thought were funny. A few years out in the "real world" certainly changes the way you look at life.

A special speaker came to lecture our class on poetry. He had a list of what he said were the most important poems. I asked him whose list it was, as I didn't agree that these were the "most important." He stuttered around for a bit and then said, "Well, it's my list." If I had been back in regular high school, I would have never been brave enough to question his authority, yet being a thirty-year-old woman gave me not only a different perspective but the ability to voice my opinions.

When I finally received my diploma, I was surprised it didn't have the meaning for me that I thought it would. But, no matter, what, I actually did enjoy going to school and being in a classroom again.

On the last night of school, however, an empty feeling suddenly swept over me. I became disoriented. Confused. It was a mental block of some sort, but I was at least coherent enough to know I could absolutely NOT drive home. The history teacher volunteered to drive me. He said he was worried that something was going on mentally with me. Apparently, finishing high school was not all that was bothering me.

Patty started tap and ballet lessons in about the second grade. It was there I met Evelynn Green, who brought her daughter to tap lessons too. Evelynn and her husband, Don, were to become our best friends as the girls continued their schooling.

We went on Sunday picnics and hikes together in the summer, and in the winter, we went ice skating, sometimes at Lake Pactolus and sometimes at Evergreen. Don played the piano by ear, and we would all go to their home and stand around the piano and sing and read from the *101 Best Poems* book.

Our square dancing group started as a result of conversations with Evelynn at the tap dance class. We started talking about square dancing and thought it sounded like fun. The plan: Bob and Gladys Ipson, Toby and Kay Oliver, Evelynn and Don Green, and Harold and I would form our own square, all of us beginners at square dancing. Getting the husbands to go along, however, would take some trickery. Each of the wives had to convince her husband that he was the only holdout, stating that the other husbands were eager to participate. Soon, we had our square. After we started dancing, the husbands put their heads together and discovered they had each been told the same "solitary holdout" story, but by that time, they were having fun and were quite happy to be there.

We were all novices and not great dancers, so it took a while for our square to learn to follow the calls. One of the men consistently mixed up allemande left and right with left grand, which was not part of the dance. Every time Don Green met him, he just shook his hand and danced on by. We laughed a lot. One time, the caller was watching our square and asked, "Did I call that?" Quite often, he would say, "The other left hand."

I sewed a black-and-silver shirt for Harold and a two-piece dress for myself. It took a lot of silver rickrack and time to make, but well worth the effort since we wore them a lot. We eventually improved enough to be intermediate level dancers. We even started attending dances with other groups and other callers. Occasionally, we would take the girls dancing. Harold would dance with Amy, and I would dance the Varsuvian ("Put your little foot, put your little foot, put your little foot right there,") with Patty.

Over the years, the feed business had changed; they not only sold feed for farm animals but also lawn and garden supplies. Harold opened a lawnmower and small engine repair shop within the store, drawing on the experience he'd had at Saline Feed in Denver. He sold and serviced a lot of Toro lawnmowers and McCulloch chain saws.

A colleague of his, Barney Shirane, who lived in Arvada, suggested we look at a house for sale across the street from him. It had been on the market for quite a while, he explained, and he thought we might be able to negotiate a good price. We came, we looked, we bought. The purchase price was $21,000, and the monthly payments were $126.

It was a nice brick, three-level home with four bedrooms and a basement. Financially, it was a big step for us, as we were currently living in a place where we rented out part of the house, counting on that rent to make our house payment. In the new house, we would have to manage the payments on our own. But after a series of bad renters we questioned whether it was worth the headache, and this move would put Harold's work very close to home.

My life had all the ingredients of a "happily ever after" fairytale. My neighbor pointed out one day when I was feeling down, "You have a beautiful home, a husband who loves you, and two sweet little girls. What more could you want?"

She was right, of course. But it only added guilt to my blues. I was sinking. Some mornings I could barely get out of bed. Some mornings I didn't. I looked at my life and felt like it belonged to someone else, someone more deserving, someone who would be better at mothering my girls, someone who would be the perfect wife Harold wanted me to be.

They'd all be better off if I were dead. There, I'd finally said it. I started thinking a lot about dying. A lot.

Harold noticed and started to worry. A lot. He wanted me to talk to someone, so he took me to see Dr. Matthews, the pastor at Wheat Ridge Methodist Church. He gave us what seemed like the standard pastor advice. Then one Sunday at church, as we were sitting in the pew, I felt myself being lifted up and was looking down on the rest of the congregation. It was quite frightening. The next time we met with Pastor Matthew, I told him about my out-of-body experience, sobbing the whole time. He felt it would be a good idea for me to seek professional help, so he lined up an interview with the team at Fort Logan, the mental institution in South Denver.

It was the beginning of what would be a grueling two-year journey back to normal. For starters, it meant a daily thirty-mile round trip from our home to Fort Logan for group therapy and treatment.

CHAPTER 9

FORT LOGAN

It was 1971 when I first walked into the Colorado Mental Health Institute at Fort Logan. To say I was uneasy about meeting with the Fort Logan team would have been the understatement of the year. The evaluation began with a physical examination. I cried uncontrollably and insisted I didn't belong there with all those crazy people. The doctor pointed out that it was the staff I was looking at, not patients.

"If you had broken your leg, you would need help fixing it, and now you need help fixing your mind," he explained.

That helped me to understand and accept it better. But I was still embarrassed that I couldn't fix it myself. To me, mental problems meant you couldn't manage your own life. According to my math, lack of control = stupid.

During my time there, three different patients did commit

suicide—one was a psychologist, one a school teacher, and one an engineer. Obviously, these were not stupid people, only people who couldn't handle their lives.

At first, I had trouble trying to figure out just who was on the staff and who were the patients, as the staff dressed in regular street clothes. The days were spent in group therapy and playing lots of volleyball. "Keep moving" was a big part of our treatment.

One of the patients, Mary, always kept her head down and never spoke to anyone, but every morning I would say, "Good morning, Mary." She never gave any indication she ever heard or saw me. Months later, she brought a woman over to meet me, introduced her as her mother-in-law, and said, "This is my friend, Betty." Everyone was surprised. These were the first words anyone had heard her speak.

For over a year, I made the forty-mile roundtrip drive five days a week for therapy and treatment but couldn't see any progress. I fell back into my old way of acting and feeling like the world would be a better place if I weren't in it. I was failing my family, food repulsed me, and I just couldn't eat. I had absolutely no energy and no desire to participate in anything that was going on. The staff felt I was suicidal and recommended putting me on twenty-four-hour watch in the facility. Life became easier because I didn't have any decisions to make, no cooking or paying bills.

I was in twenty-four-hour care for about a month. To get off twenty-four-hour care, I had to go before the staff and convince them I was stable enough to live on the "outside." I looked around at the people who were staying there—many of whom were in and out often—and decided that it would be much too easy to let myself be taken care of and not have any responsibilities. I was afraid that I would become like them if I were to stay. So I asked for, and was granted, a return to daily care.

During this time, Harold came out to family night once every two weeks, when the families and counselors discussed what was going on with the patients and them. He was surprised at the kinds of problems families had. He also learned that the one seeking help wasn't the only one who needed it.

"It was the first time I looked at my own behavior and saw how I was contributing to her problems," Harold confessed to a friend. "I quit trying to mold her into my idea of the perfect wife and let Betty be Betty."

One time, my parents came with him to one of the family group sessions. They couldn't understand why this had happened, and they wanted a short, quick answer. Why hadn't it been fixed yet? This opened a door for a rather lengthy discussion. I think they left with a little better understanding of how these things worked.

Toward the end of two years, the staff felt it would be beneficial for me to have private counseling with a psychologist closer to home before I would be ready to leave Fort Logan. Harold and I had weekly sessions with Dr. Wilson in Lakewood. It was very helpful for the two of us to go together and discuss ongoing problems we weren't even aware of. The sessions opened the door for better communication.

One of the problems was that Harold thought I was spending too much money. I had always paid the bills and took care of the financial end of our marriage. Dr. Wilson suggested that Harold take over paying the bills; then he could see just where the money was going. That helped tremendously. When Harold was angry with me, he wouldn't speak for days. Dr. Wilson suggested he might just throw a bucket of water on me and get on with life. Anything was better than the silent treatment.

At Fort Logan I was issued a great many medications. Some were to pick me up, and others were to calm me down. They said I would need to take them for the rest of my life. One day I looked down at the lot of them, carried them out to the incinerator, and threw away the entire bunch. I have not taken any mood-altering medications since.

About that time, Georgia, an employee at the feed store, loaned me the Dale Carnegie book *How to Win Friends and Influence People.* I was unable to focus long enough to do any serious reading, but in the first few pages of this book it suggested we learn to live in "day-tight compartments" with no past and no future beyond twenty-four hours. I learned to do this so well that when I was brushing my teeth I brushed up and I brushed down. When I was bathing, I washed my left arm ... my left hand ... my left fingers. Then the right side—always living "in the moment." Even sorting rice became a beautiful event. Today they call it "mindfulness."

I was able to achieve this so completely that later, when we decided to plant a green ash tree in our front yard, I realized it was the first time in months I'd thought in terms of the future, and it was a bit of a shock. Planting a tree is the quintessential symbol of belief in the future. I was starting to plan ahead. The tree did not flourish the first year, and that was frightening. But after a year or so, it did well. I guess, like me, it was finding it rough adapting to its new reality.

I had a similar moment that Christmas at the candlelight service at the Arvada Methodist Church when Dr. Hanna said, "Let this flame be a symbol of your life, and let it shine in the world."

I looked down and realized my candle had no wick. Oh NO! Did this mean I had no flame, no life, no future? However (and there is always a however), the next year my candle had TWO wicks and flamed like a blowtorch. Another symbol? A sign? Or just a coincidence?

Speaking of signs, I once sat down to my regular meditation. And because I had some swelling in my ankles and feet, I decided to soak my feet in a nice, warm Epsom salt bath as I meditated. Our teacher told us that it was traditional after the meditation to ask for an unexpected sign that we are on the right track. So I did.

As I was lifting my feet, I discovered a tiny mouse floating face down in the water. This was a sign I definitely had not expected. We have lived in this house for over twenty-four years and have never seen a mouse, dead or alive, either before or after that one. I couldn't help laughing. Maybe next time I should ask for something slightly more traditional.

My time at Fort Logan was quite disruptive to our family. The girls were teenagers and had no one to listen to their concerns. Barney's wife, Sue Shirane, who lived across the street from us, was very helpful to them.

After I left Fort Logan, Harold's sister Nelline and I attended drapery making classes at adult ed and started our own drapery business. We called it Window Wise Draperies. We carried books of samples, measured and bid jobs, made the drapes in our basement, and then delivered and hung them. It was going well, and we were steadily attracting new customers.

But working in the basement for so many hours a day proved to be not so good for my recovery. I felt myself sinking back into depression. Dr. Wilson suggested that I either hire someone to make the drapes so I could get out with customers doing the continued selling and measuring or get out of the business—which I did. Nelline carried on for a couple of years after I left.

CHAPTER 10

DAIRY QUEEN

Harold had a long relationship with the Willis family. They gave him his first job when he was eighteen, which allowed us to get married. But Harold found himself in a tricky position when one of the Willis family members who was working for him created an impossible situation where Harold couldn't work with him and couldn't fire him because of his family ties. Then they decided that they would sell the store to Harold, but the process dragged on with one delay after another. The bank said they needed more information, and the family kept postponing the delivery of the papers they requested.

Finally, we arranged to meet with them to discuss the final plans. After we had discussed the weather, the family, and current events, they told us they decided not to sell, as they didn't feel Harold was capable of running the store. This was especially hurtful, as Harold had been effectively running the store for ten years and had until recently had a good relationship with the family.

It was like a blow to the stomach. He had gone to a lot of trouble to get the bank loan together. We had made plans and promises. Before we arrived home, he decided he couldn't work for them under these circumstances. The next day he gave his two-week notice.

It was a difficult time, as he had worked for the Willises for twenty-one years, since he left high school, and had never had to look for work. He read ads and tried to decide what it was he really wanted to do. He was offered jobs with several different companies that would have required a lot of travel or a move out of town, neither of which appealed to him.

About this time, he walked into our local Dairy Queen, which was just across a small park from where we lived. The owner, Bob Alison, told him the lawnmower he had repaired for him was working better than when it was new. Harold told Bob about the store purchase falling through, and that he was looking for a job. Bob asked him to come and work at the Dairy Queen, but Harold wasn't sure.

So Bob said, "Come over and work with me, and if you like it then we'll talk about selling it to you."

After a couple of months, Bob suggested that Harold manage the store for him so he could get out and develop more stores, as he had the franchise for the whole Denver area. So Harold managed the store for about a year and a half, and then Bob offered us a more than fair deal to purchase the place.

Our parents—both sets—gave us no encouragement. My dad asked once if we were still interested in buying "that hamburger joint." Harold's folks showed no interest in the store or our decision.

We talked it over and weighed the pros and cons. Finally, it seemed to come down to knowing we had to do something and acknowledging that the Alisons had made us a very, very good offer. Harold had already talked to the bank, and he felt he was prepared to own his own business. If there were cons, they never came up. So we became the owners of the neighborhood Dairy Queen.

But before we even started with the Dairy Queen, I was hit with another challenge. I had not been feeling well. My doctors called for a battery of tests and pronounced the verdict: I had thyroid cancer. Everyone imagines how they would react to such news. Well, I can tell you, being told you have cancer is one of the most devastating pronouncements you will ever hear. I immediately thought of the long months at Fort Logan when I felt as if I didn't want to live and then getting my life back together again, only to hear I might not live—well, it was quite a shock. I was thirty-eight years old.

When they operated, they found it was two kinds of cancer, papillary and follicular, with the very real possibility it might have spread outside the original site; I needed another operation to remove a major muscle the cancer might have invaded. The decision to have another operation so soon after the first one was difficult, but the doctor convinced me that it might be the only way to save my life. So six weeks later, I had a radical neck dissection. They did not find more cancer, so nothing more was done at that time—no radiation or chemotherapy. This was in 1969, and I don't know how much of this postoperative treatment they did then.

The insurance we had at that time was for "catastrophic illness." The company canceled our policy as soon as they found it was cancer. What's more catastrophic than cancer?

The Alisons couldn't have been more fair and helpful than they were during that time. Mary Lou even came back and worked for us while we went to Minneapolis for DQ training. She told us how pleased they were to have us running the store.

At the training sessions we learned how the parent company wanted the stores run, and we tried hard to follow their rules and suggestions. The mix for the product (we were to call it "Dairy Queen," not "ice cream") was produced according to their specifications at the Robinson Dairy in Denver. Harold would drive there and pick up the mix a couple of times a week. The mixture was a low-fat product and had very little, if any, cream in it.

We always used the best toppings available. We found that strawberries from the state of Washington were the very best, so we always bought frozen berries in five-gallon containers. After visiting some local DQs, we found not everyone saw things the way we did. One store in a small town north of us had jars of pineapple toppings that were filled two-thirds with simple syrup and one-third with pineapple—just barely flavored sugar syrup.

The Alisons' crews had been made up of three adult women and boys from the local high school. The Alisons found it too difficult to work with boys and girls together, so they just kept it to boys. Their own three boys worked there. The crews were well-trained and experienced, so we kept them on and hired more as we needed them.

I had told Harold the DQ was his and I was not going to work there, as I didn't feel we should or could work together. But after I quit the drapery business, I told him, "If you want, I have the time now and can handle your employee scheduling." He took me up on it. One day, after a very busy lunch hour, Harold threatened to close and lock the doors if I didn't schedule him more help. I went home, changed clothes, came back, and went to work for the next fifteen years.

After I began making out the schedule and doing most of the training, we developed some specific policies. We felt it was important that the young people not only learn how to make the products but also learn work habits that would serve them throughout their lives, no matter what kinds of jobs they had as adults. We scheduled around their school functions to the best of our ability, unless they started wanting more time off than they wanted to work. We expected them to be on time for their scheduled shift, be clean, keep the place clean, and treat the customers and us honestly and fairly.

When our employees were asked how we were to work for, many years after they left the DQ, several of them said we were tough but fair. They were proud of the store where they had worked. One of our boys (who later went into police work) said he still can't walk into a DQ without noticing if it is run the way we ran things. Another (who became a financial advisor) came back and told us he'd learned more about handling people working at the DQ than he did in all of his years of college. Not many stores measured up to our standards.

We also made it a point never to criticize or correct them in front of customers. One very nervous young man was making a cone for a customer when I walked behind him and said, "Dan, when you're through there, I need to see you in back." The cone jerked sideways, and it was the crookedest, oddest looking cone I had ever seen.

Afterwards, he walked to the back room, put his hand on his hip, and said, "Mrs. Payte, don't ever talk to me when I'm making a cone."

I'd only wanted to talk to him about scheduling, but I found it very hard to keep from laughing.

We had contests from time to time to keep the boys interested in selling. We took them out for breakfast and had cookouts occasionally, and that seemed to be something they strived for. One time we found one of the boys running out to a car with a bag of Dilly® Bars. One of his sales pitches was: "How about a bag of Dilly Bars for your home freezer?" But he had forgotten to ask while they were in the store. He grew up to be a banker.

Making too many mistakes got to be a problem, so we had a contest to see if we could have seven days without any employee mistakes. They worked very hard to make that happen. We found out eventually that one of them had been making chocolate malts any time he couldn't remember what had been ordered. That explained the abundance of chocolate malts we found in the freezer!

This was before automated cash registers, so everyone had to learn how to make change. We hired a science teacher from the high school to work part-time for us in the evenings and weekends. He was a very bright young man, but making change

Harold and Betty's first Dairy Queen on Wadsworth and 64th
Arvada, Colorado, 1970

didn't make any sense to him. I took him and a change drawer into the back room, closed the door, and we worked at making change for different orders. The light finally dawned for him, and the problem was solved. He helped us find good help at the high school, and he made sure they knew how to make change when they started.

On one occasion, we asked one of the boys to change the reader board out front while we were gone. We didn't tell him what to say. His first reader board said: "Dairy Queen—Where You Can Eat Dirt Cheap." "No, Gary, take that down now!" we told him, trying to emphasize the purpose of the reader board. Then he suggested, "Whoppers cause constipation." With that suggestion, we never asked him to change the board again.

The hours were long. Most of the time, we opened the store in the morning, worked through the lunch hour, and then returned in the evening to close the store—seven days a week. There were days I couldn't tell you what day it was, but I knew we had to mix a batch of strawberry topping that day.

After a couple of years of this, Harold and I took a day off and decided to go to Estes Park for the day. We stopped at roadside parks once on the way there and twice on the way back to take naps. We were that bone tired.

About the time we bought the Dairy Queen, Patty went away to college, so she never worked there. Amy showed no interest in working there either, but we were not thrilled to have her home alone and wondering where she was while we were gone so much. We told her she was going to work at the Dairy Queen, but she was adamant, "I don't want to work at the Dairy Queen." So we compromised: she would work there until she found a job somewhere else so we would know where she was. We even discussed turning the store over to her to manage if she didn't want to go on to college.

That all changed when she signed on with the Arvada High School Band. The band was planning a trip to Europe the following year. The band members were expected to pay their own expenses, and Amy started working at the DQ with new resolve. She took every spare shift anyone offered and saved every penny. She went to Europe with the Arvada High School Band. And when she graduated, she chose college.

For three years, we worked day in and day out, perfecting our DQ in Arvada. So when the DQ in Northglenn, roughly twelve miles away, came up for sale, we thought we were ready to take on another one and bought it.

Retraining the employees was quite a challenge, as this store came to us with a lot of bad habits. The boss dressed the girls in hot pants and seemed more interested in attracting young male customers—not exactly "the DQ way." One customer complained, "Since you bought the store, you've taken all the sex out of it." Our answer: "Thank you!"

After we purchased the Northglenn Dairy Queen, we heard that the little walk-up DQ in Wheat Ridge was also being sold by a couple who wanted to retire. They already had a buyer, but when he went to the bank for a loan, the bank said the store's records didn't support the price they were asking. Harold knew how much mix they were using and how much money they should be taking in based on that figure. It looked to us like they might have been pocketing some of the income without reporting their real sales. It helped us to know the truth of the operation, and we were able to deal from that place. We also had some money left over from the loan we'd taken out to buy the Northglenn store.

Since we were going into an existing store, we expected to spend some time training the existing employees up to our standards. For example, they cut up the banana in little bite-size pieces for banana splits as opposed to the long slice—they felt that would make them easier to eat. ARGHHH!

By this time, we had to hire managers for the new stores, since we couldn't manage all of them ourselves. So I took the plunge and became a manager. And to my great surprise, I was rather a natural at managing both staff and customers.

Customers would line up outside, allowing me an opportunity to greet each one personally. We had one man, Boyce, who was wheelchair-bound, but he would pull up, wrestle his chair out of the car, and repeat the process all over again just to dump his trash.

One day he came to the window and said, "I have a question."

My reply, "I have an answer."

Boyce asked, "What's the answer?"

"Seven and a half. What's the question?"

"What's my dad's hat size?" he replied.

One of the neighboring businessmen was always looking for a way to get something for less than the going price. On Mother's Day, we always had "Mom's treat" for half price. I could see him walking across the parking lot with a kind of smile on his face. I knew he had something in mind.

He walked up to the window and said, "Hi, I'm the mother of invention."

So, of course, he got his treat for half price. We had fun. It was those kinds of connection that created repeat customers and made everyone feel good.

Our fourth and final purchase of a Dairy Queen was an old filling station for sale in Commerce City. We bought this in partnership with Jim Lemmon, another DQ operator, then had it remodeled into a Dairy Queen. Before any remodeling could begin, the old gas tanks in the ground had to be removed. So our first expense was over $5,000. The store went on to be quite successful, and eventually we sold our half to our manager, Carl.

It was interesting to observe the buying habits of the customers in the four different locations. Northglenn and Commerce City were busy and generous on payday, and when welfare checks arrived, even the three-year-olds got banana splits—which they couldn't finish. Later in the month, business dropped off significantly. In Arvada, even if a little kid wanted a banana split, he got a small cone or a Dilly Bar. Their business continued at a pretty even rate throughout the month. The 44th Street store, the little walk-up, attracted a lot of elderly people and teenagers. They were not big spenders but continued to come unless the weather got too cold.

The previous owners always closed for the winter and went south, but we kept it open all year. It took a while for the customers to adjust to that schedule. We also offered hot dogs and barbecue beef sandwiches to entice them to stop in on some very cold nights. I think we must have looked very lonely in there at times. On some nights I brought a good book. And since there was always something to clean or do in a Dairy Queen, on other nights that's exactly what we did.

Most of our neighborhood chats, while we lived in Arvada, seemed to take place in the middle of the street. There were four or five neighbors who would just stand around and discuss the topic of the day.

One day, the focus was on our neighbor Deloris and her son Leland, who was planning to get married. Deloris said she was thinking of wearing a pantsuit to her son's wedding. As you might imagine, there was more than one school of thought on that subject. After the conversation, I went inside to do my yoga lessons, as I was taking classes at Metro College and needed to practice. The yoga went well, and when I was done, I just lay on the floor in a very relaxed Shavasana position with my arms lying loosely on the floor at my side. In my very relaxed position, I idly asked the question, "I wonder what God thinks about wearing a pantsuit to a wedding?"

The answer came immediately and forcefully: "Thou shalt love the Lord thy God, with all thy heart, with all thy soul, with all thy mind and thy neighbor as thyself."

I shook 'til my teeth rattled. I hadn't expected such a commanding answer. Apparently, God really doesn't care what you wear to the wedding, as long as you love Him, your neighbor, and yourself. This was a great life lesson for me: Who is this God? Who is this neighbor? Who is myself? The rest of my life has been the search for the answers to these questions.

CHAPTER 11

SCUBA DIVING

O ur scuba diving adventures started in about 1980. We had been on a trip to Hawaii and tried a little snorkeling. The water was pretty rough, so that first try was not much fun, just enough to pique our interest. Later we flew with Ports of Call, a travel club out of Denver, to Eleuthera, a small island in the Bahamas, and tried it again.

The water was a beautiful aqua blue, and it was warm. Perfect for falling in love with snorkeling. But I was scared. I didn't trust that the water would hold me up. Harold held my hand to calm me down and ease myself under the water. I'm not sure why holding his hand made me feel safe, but it worked. It always worked.

When I got past the scary part of putting my head under the water and started to feel comfortable, oh, what a beautiful new world there was to discover! We saw waving sea fans and small schools of fish of every imaginable color. I simply HAD to go down and sit with the fish myself.

When we were back home, Amy and Jim mentioned that they had just signed up for scuba lessons in Lakewood. Scuba diving was an entirely different level than snorkeling, but what the heck, we decided to join them. Just one tiny hurdle: I couldn't swim.

I went to our local YMCA and asked about swimming lessons. At the first class, they gave us a kickboard and we were instructed to kick up and down the pool lanes. My instructor said she had never seen anyone go backwards on the kickboard before, so apparently I was starting well behind the others. I had to take that beginner class three times. But I did. And soon I was swimming half a mile up and down the pool without that darn kickboard.

Our open water certification dive was done on Grand Cayman in October 1981. I had to descend very slowly due to extreme ear pain. It was so bad that I thought I might not be able to go down at all, but the slower I went the pressure eased up. When I reached the bottom, my ears felt no pressure at all, which allowed me to be in the moment and enjoy the view. And I loved it! To see more clearly, I took off the mask and buddy breathed with Harold, sharing one mask and tank. We saw a lot of bright blue, yellow, and even a small red fish.

On April 22, 1982, Harold and I went in for our certification test. On our first dive off the Island of Bonaire, we entered the water by jumping from the boat and went down twenty-five feet. Apparently, I was extremely afraid, and every time someone jumped off, I blew more air into my buoyancy compensator. When it came to my turn, I jumped in and didn't even get my hair wet. I just bobbed around like a cork, not even realizing what was happening. Harold said it was very funny to watch me.

Eventually, we dived to a depth of 120 feet and even did a night dive—pretty scary to turn your light around and see what is following you. One time, a moray eel swam up from between my arms right in front of me. They swim with their mouths open and sharp teeth showing. Yikes! I still had some ear problems, and by then my nose was bleeding, filling my mask with blood. I eventually had to give up diving because of the bloody nose problem. Despite the obvious, it turns out one shouldn't be in the water swimming amongst the sharks with blood all over them.

CHAPTER 12

VOLUNTEERING

During the years of our over-the-top crazy schedule running four Dairy Queens, we remained members of the Arvada Methodist Church, which kept us happily busy in community work. Harold and I were always on the lookout for opportunities to serve. Our first effort was with third-grade girls who needed help learning to read.

The second group was students from a Denver school who also needed help with their reading. Amy had a third-grade girl from that group, and I had a sixth-grade boy. I dreaded working with a sixth-grade boy, as I felt he might resent my attempt to help. But he seemed to welcome my efforts, and after a visit with his family I could understand why. The support at home was pretty nonexistent, and he was on his own. We got his grade up from an F to a B, and he was very happy.

My next volunteer project was with the Probation Department in Jefferson County. At the indoctrination meeting, I listened to them describe what alcoholic behavior is, and I could see myself in the same situation—only I didn't drink. The way it worked: I would meet with the client once a week in their home, then report what was going on in their world. More than anything, though, people need someone to talk with.

The first client was a German transplant whose husband had left her with three children. She then had a new boyfriend and another baby on the way. I went with her to her court hearing to explain that yes, she had been picked up for drunk driving, but she had been under tremendous stress and was genuinely remorseful, and I was confident it wouldn't happen again. If she wasn't scared straight just being in court, she definitely was when the judge got through with us. I had the feeling if she was ever caught drunk driving again, we would both be thrown in jail.

I came to realize that she was a very clever and resourceful individual. For instance, when her car fan belt broke, she took the one from her washing machine and put it in her car. It worked. When her probation time was up, we were both sorry to see the end of our weekly sessions.

The next client was a woman who had stolen alcohol from a drugstore in Golden. One night, she called me from the hospital and wanted us to pick her up. Her husband had beaten her up and she was in the hospital for X-rays and tests and was ready to come home. She wanted us to stop at Ace-Hi Tavern to check on her husband. Harold put his foot down and said, "No way."

I went to court with her on one occasion, and her daughter was also there for a court appearance because she had beaten up her husband. Her two cute under-teenage boys were arrested for stealing bicycles. The whole family needed HELP.

Another probationer was arrested for stealing from the store where she worked. It soon became clear her husband was behind the whole plot. When we were meeting in her home, he made it a point to be there every time. At the end of our time together, he seemed to be okay with everything and said he was sorry to see the sessions end.

As a small business in the community, we became active in the local Rotary Club and specifically their program of welcoming and hosting foreign exchange students. While we were running the Dairy Queens, we had three different Rotary exchange students live with us.

Claus Lowgren from Sweden was our first guest. The policy of the Rotary Club then was to have the students stay at each home for six weeks, then move on to the next home. Claus was an easy keeper who enjoyed doing whatever we were doing—in addition to the ski trips he was able to take to the mountains. He constantly wanted to try new things. We had a deal with him that once a week he could go over to the DQ and have a free treat. Each time, he picked something he had never had before. When he went skiing, he couldn't afford to buy lunch there, so he would get a bunch of ketchup packages and add them to hot water for tomato soup.

The students were pretty much left to themselves in their upstairs bedroom, and I had them bring down the sheets once a week so I could wash them. One time, Claus brought down his sheets, overwhelmed by embarrassment. He held up the sheet and said, "The sheet, the sheet, the sheet—it broke." Obviously, it was not a new sheet, and it had split when he turned over.

I was going to Weight Watchers then and made a rather limp chocolate pudding, which he ate, but he called it my "psychological pudding." Many years later, he came back and visited us again, twice.

The following year, we hosted Freddie Santos from the Philippines. Freddie was a whole different experience. We never considered that any of them might be smokers, but Freddie was. He was raised in a household with servants and had never even made his own bed. So we were a whole different experience for him too. One of the things that impressed us was how he was never taught to pick up any food with his fingers; he could cut the meat off a chicken bone as cleanly as if it had been boiled.

Freddie loved opera music and would sit in the living room listening to his records and applaud and shout for the performances. We took him to the play *1776* in Central City, and at the end he stood up and shouted, "Director! Director!"—the only one in the whole theater who did. Amy was mortified.

We let him work at the Dairy Queen a little because it sounded like fun to him, and he made it that way. When he would pass out a spoon to a customer, he would say something like, "You get a blue spoon because you have blue eyes."

He had a comment for everyone. The other employees thought him very odd. We were not allowed to pay him anything for his work, so we decided to buy him a winter coat, as he was always cold and wore brown jersey gloves around all the time. We scouted the whole shopping center looking for the perfect coat, only to have him decide that the first coat he tried on was "the one." It had a fur collar, and he said, "Yup, it's the real me."

He loved anything soft and furry and bought us four rabbit

skins to put onto the back of our sofa. When it was time for him to move on, he kissed the side of our house and said he loved his time there—the King of Drama! Freddie also came back to visit us a couple of times in later years.

Our third exchange student was a girl from Zimbabwe, Heather Masterson. She stayed with us for double the usual time, as she had observed the next family she was to stay with and didn't want to live with them. That suited us just fine, as we really enjoyed having her, and we had fun shopping and sewing together. She made herself a wool suit that she loved wearing here, but when she got home to Zimbabwe, it was totally inappropriate—no need for anything that warm there. She also bought a down sleeping bag, which also couldn't be used there.

We took Heather on a couple of cross-country ski trips in Winter Park, which she loved. She had never seen snow before and couldn't believe that those great piles of snow came from such little flakes. When it came time for her to leave and go back home, it was a very tearful leaving. We felt as if we had lost a member of the family, and I was unable to go into her room for three days after she left.

Several years later, we visited her in Zimbabwe. This was after she was married and had two little girls. We had a wonderful time there, visiting places that most tourists don't get to see. We spent three days on their boat on Lake Kariba and went to Victoria Falls, the ruins of Great Zimbabwe, and on a daily safari to see the animals in the wild. One place had many petroglyphs, drawn over hundreds of years by different tribes. One tribe would come in and take over that territory, only to be conquered by the next marauding group, and each left their mark. The petroglyphs look just like the petroglyphs around Colorado.

Many years after, we were visiting with her on the phone, and I mentioned I would just love to sit and talk with her over a cup of tea. The next day, she called back and said she hoped I meant it, as she had called and bought a plane ticket to come back to Colorado and visit. What a happy surprise!

Our next set of foreign guests came to us from the Hospitality Group. The first was a couple from Paris. They didn't stay very long, and my most vivid memory of their visit was the wife doing cartwheels in the yard with a dress on.

The second set was a couple of Japanese girls. They were with us a little longer, and we got to know them better. They really wanted to ride horses, so we took them on an outing to Grand Lake where they could ride in the mountains. We stopped on the way and had a pancake breakfast over a campfire. They had never been on a picnic before and seemed to enjoy the whole idea of doing something so new to them. One of them noted how close the stars seemed to be, and how easy it was to point out all the constellations. Red Rocks was one of their favorite places. Another commented on our Cadillac. They said it was like "riding around in a room."

CHAPTER 13

TAKING FLIGHT

After sixteen years of nose-to-the-grindstone in Dairy Queens, Harold was growing tired of managing staff and the endless exhausting hours. When one of his managers so much as hinted at interest in buying the Arvada store, Harold jumped at the chance. Sold. Shortly afterward, the second store was sold, then the third. Over the span of the year 1986, all four stores were sold, and Harold and I found ourselves both relieved and ready for another chapter. But what?

One morning shortly after the last DQ sold, I was reading the paper and noted an ad about flying lessons at the nearby Jeffco airport.

Could I?

Nahhh.

But.

Maybe I could.

I grabbed my coat, tucked the paper under my arm, and started heading for the door.

"What are you doing today?" Harold asked.

"I thought I'd go learn how to fly."

"Hmm," he said, almost used to my ways at this point. He then went to grab his coat, and said, "I want to learn to fly, too. I'm going with you."

My fascination with flying goes way back. Yet, I can't seem to remember exactly when it started. Suffice to say, it was way back before I ordered Captain Midnight's cardboard cockpit control panel setup so I could be his pretend copilot while I listened to the program. I always wanted to fly, even after my cousin died during his homecoming trip with his airplane. Maybe it's a family gene.

We went to the airport in Jeffco to check on flying lessons and were directed to Jerry Nolan, the owner of Denver Air Center. He suggested we buy a plane, and he would include lessons for both of us, as well as Amy and her new husband, Jim. He explained that we could lease back the plane to generate some income. After selling the DQs, we were looking for an investment with some kind of tax credit, and this seemed to fit the bill. And it would be fun at the same time!

Learning to fly wasn't easy for me. I really was starting from ground zero. At one point, Joe, the instructor, told me to "do a 180," and I had no idea what that meant. He asked if my mother hadn't taught me about that sort of thing, and I couldn't remember if she even knew what a compass was.

When I passed my ground school test with a good grade,

I shouted and cried for at least an hour. I learned to analyze weather reports, how to read a flight map, and many other things I never knew.

When I went to get my flight physical, the doctor was concerned that I'd had cancer and almost didn't let me pass. I thought that was a crazy reason not to be licensed to fly. I could understand if you had heart problems that might come on as a sudden, unexpected attack, but it would require some pretty precise planning to die of cancer while flying a plane. I did some fast talking to get him to pass me.

During my flight lessons I hated to see that ground coming up at me when it was time to land. Joe explained the obvious: that I had to get closer to the land because I couldn't stay in the air forever. He also suggested I not use the term "point of impact" when we were approaching the proposed landing spot. Picky, picky!

When it came time for me to do my first solo flight around the field, we were at the Erie Airfield. We had made several "touch and goes," when Joe said he was getting out and I was to take the plane up by myself. Now, Joe was a really big fellow, and when he got out of the plane, it lifted off the ground like a rocket. What a shock! We were both pleased when I made it down again safely, proving that old flying truism: any landing you can walk away from is a good landing.

Harold and I went to the airport several times a week and even did some night flying. I learned how to do stalls and how to recover from them—not my favorite thing, but I could do it.

On my first long-distance solo flight, I flew the forty-minute flight to Colorado Springs, then another forty-five minutes on to Lamar and back to JeffCo Airport. While flying over Golden, I glanced down at the TV towers and thought to myself, "Betty, what are you doing in this little plane all by yourself; why are you not home knitting?" Then I remembered: My mother tried to teach me to knit, and I just couldn't seem to catch on.

I called Flight Service and told them of my plans to head to Jeffco so they could give me the headings they wanted me to fly. They were quite busy, and at first, routed me a long way around Denver. Later, they called back and said traffic had cleared enough, so they sent me straight across Denver. We had been taught to always look for a place to land, in case you lost an engine, so as I was flying across Downtown Denver, looking down at all those tall buildings, none of it looked remotely like a place to land. Then I spotted the golf course and decided that would be the best emergency landing option. Fortunately, I didn't lose an engine and made it safely back to our home airport. WHEW! The only casualty in the whole experience was a flight map.

One day, as we approached our home airport, we heard a shaky, young voice over the radio talking to the tower, saying he was lost and needed help getting home. The tower said, very calmly and gently, "We are not able to hear your total message, as you are not holding the talk button down on your mike." The young man said, "I'm a student pilot," about three times, to which the tower responded, "We understand that, but you need to hold the button down, and then we can direct you home." We didn't hear of any plane crashes, so we assume he made it back safely.

Just before it was time for us to test for our licenses, I got cold feet and thought I would just quit. One of the instructors took me up to the mountains, shut off the engine, and said, "Now, isn't that quieter?" He somehow convinced me that I did know how to fly, so I continued on toward our licenses.

It was July 25, 1983 when we got our licenses. I did my check ride first, firmly establishing that I am the senior pilot in this family. Harold got his about an hour later. When I was flying with the tester, the hood was blocking my field of vision, which made me nervous. I asked him if he was looking out for other air traffic. He said he was, and I got my license anyway. He even said I was a safe pilot. Yay!

Over the next five years, we regularly took trips on the plane. Some of the first ones were treasure hunts that the Denver Air Center dreamed up. They would give us clues, and we would have to figure out what the destination was, fly there, get our card stamped, and then go on to breakfast at the last stop. We flew to both Cheyenne, WY, and Saratoga, WY, for breakfast, then back home. The Saratoga Inn would pick us up at the airport, drive us to the inn for breakfast, and then drive us back. Cheyenne was always windy, but the restaurants were within walking distance of the airport, and we would walk to those.

On one of the trips to Saratoga, it had snowed, and I had to land on a snow-covered runway. I gripped the yoke tightly, and if it wasn't so cold I would have been sweating, but the snowy landing was very soft, almost like landing on a pillow. One of the most fun trips we flew was to Rock Springs, WY, to pick up my sister, who was visiting friends there. Our flight took us over the many small towns in Wyoming, so separated from each other that I wondered if they felt as lonely and isolated as they looked from up on the plane.

Betty and Harold taking a flying lesson in 1981

We were once asked to ferry a couple of new small planes from Wichita, KS, where they had been manufactured. They flew us there, we picked up the new planes, and flew them back to Jeffco. It felt good to be trusted to fly the new planes back. And we did it!

We flew to Kansas often to pick up our grandsons and bring them back to Colorado. They especially liked to fly with us when it was time for our annual flight review and we had to do stalls. They thought the stalls were a lot of fun.

Other times were not so much fun. One trip, returning from Kansas City, we had the plane fueled up and expected to land in Garden City with over half a tank of fuel. We ran into a headwind the likes of which we had never experienced before. The fuel numbers were dropping like crazy, and the cars on the ground were traveling faster than we were. We made it back safely and felt like it was finally safe to exhale. There were other times when I seriously looked for a field where we might be forced to land because we were running low on fuel or worried about bad weather, but fortunately, we had no crashes or even close calls. And, best of all, it fulfilled one of my lifelong dreams.

After we'd had the plane for five years or so, Joe talked to us about trading in our Cessna for the French-made Tobago. It was a faster, easier plane to fly, and it was an upgrade. Of course, we do as we're told. The Tobago was a low-wing plane, so we needed additional training. It was a whole different experience from flying the Cessna. I was awarded a French airplane license but never got to France to try it out.

After eight years of flying, the novelty wore off, and the cost became more than we wanted to spend. We tried renting the plane out to different people to help with the upkeep, but that wasn't always an easy venture. When one renter neglected to refuel before heading home and was forced to make an emergency landing on South Table Mountain in Golden, we decided it was time to sell.

CHAPTER 14

THE SENTINEL

After the chaotic life of managing Dairy Queens, and the exciting life of flying planes, both Harold and I kept busy with part-time jobs. I knew myself well enough to see that I was happiest when I was doing something or learning something. So when I saw an ad in the *Jefferson Sentinel* for a receptionist, I decided to apply. I had never done anything like that before, so I wasn't surprised when I didn't get the job. They hired someone with experience. Several months later, I was cleaning up after breakfast when the phone rang.

"Hello. Payte's."

"Uh, Betty?"

"Yes?"

"Don Gorham here, From *The Sentinel.*"

"Well, hello, Mr. Gorham. What can I do for you?"

"Well, I—we—were wondering, would you still be interested in that receptionist job?

"Well, sure, I guess. What hap—?

"The other girl didn't work out. Could you come in and reapply?"

And so I did. Unfortunately, the interview didn't go well.

"How many words a minute can you type?"

"Oh, I don't know, twenty maybe?"

"Twenty!"

"Maybe twenty-five?"

"We have a ten-line phone setup. Ever worked one of those?"

"No."

"Ever manage an office?"

"No."

I started to gather my coat and purse to leave, then turned to give it one last shot. "But I managed one of our four Dairy Queen stores, I'm organized, and I work hard. And I earned my pilot's license."

I got the job. It definitely was a steep learning curve for me. I took all the phone calls for the circulation department, the salespeople, and the editorial staff. Every department had its own particular personality quirks.

The circulation people were very practical and just wanted to see the papers distributed correctly. The salespeople were more high-pressure types—always looking to get more sales leads, making sure that the ads were in on time and correctly done. They seemed to be constantly frustrated. The editorial staff, on the other hand, were laid back and interested mainly in the stories of the surrounding communities. Their defining proverbial motto was, "If the Second Coming of Jesus happened outside of Jefferson County, *The Sentinel* would not cover it."

Often people came in who wanted to have their group or event promoted without taking out ads. The editorial staff was quite selective about that—especially around election time.

While those in the circulation department were quite independent, the editorial staff personnel were cerebral and unable to do the most basic tasks—like fill the copy machine with paper. Once, one of the editors brought me a can of soup and a can opener; she didn't even know how to work the can opener.

Sure, I made mistakes as I was learning the job. One of my most important tasks was to go to the courthouse once a week and pick up the legal notices to be published in the paper the following week. I had overlooked one of the offices, and that whole set of notices didn't get into the paper for three consecutive weeks. That's right, due to my steep learning curve, meetings and deadlines had to be rearranged across Jefferson County for weeks.

Another part of my job was proofreading ads for the salespeople. United Welding took out a full-page ad filled with information on all the small jobs they did. We went over it carefully to see that the explanation of the job and the price was correct. The salesperson looked it over, then took it to the customer for him to examine, then back to me for the final okay. The whole ad was perfect, except for one minor detail (in the huge headline)—two letters were transposed, and the word "United" came out "Untied" Welding.

He was not a happy customer, and frankly, I didn't know whether to laugh or cry. Everyone seemed to agree that it was all my fault. After that debacle, I don't know why, but they kept me on the job. Working at *The Sentinel* was fun, and I met a lot of new people. Eventually, I even learned to work the ten-line phone.

In time, *The Sentinel*, combined with other local papers and moved to the Lakeside Shopping Center, which made for a much longer commute, and that was the beginning of the end of that fun chapter.

CHAPTER 15

THERAPEUTIC TOUCH

While I was still at *The Sentinel* I often heard and read about therapeutic touch. The more it showed up, the more I became intrigued. Therapeutic touch is a form of bodywork in which the practitioner works with the patient's own body energy, clearing and directing that energy toward balance and self-healing. It is one of the oldest bodywork practices and is taught in some nursing schools at prestigious universities. Research has shown that it increases hemoglobin levels when practiced regularly. Go ahead, Google it.

I took a few classes from a woman named Evelyn Altman. She was a nurse who taught therapeutic classes nearby. When I was first learning, I didn't really feel much while I was holding my hands over the patient, but one night that changed. There was a man on the table, and as I passed my hands over his stomach area, for the first time I could feel the energy in my own body. In that singular moment I understood. We are all connected.

After leaving *The Sentinel*, I saw an opportunity to delve deeper into practicing therapeutic touch. I reached out to Evelyn and asked if I could shadow her—do her laundry, clean her workroom, anything—if she would let me just observe her work. She couldn't let me do that but did allow me to see some of the patients she was working on. One day, she tested my skills on one of her clients to see if I could find where her energy was blocked. I put my hands over her and knew instantly that her left knee was the location of the blockage. Evelyn looked at me like a proud mother.

After that, Evelyn allowed me to work on different people in different locations. One was in a hospital where one fellow had lost his lower arm in a burn accident, but the arm still hurt him, even though physically there was no arm there. We worked with him for a few treatments that allowed him to "disappear" the phantom arm.

This continued for quite a while, until I decided to start my own business along with Phyllis Rice, one of the salespeople at *The Sentinel*. She agreed to do the paperwork and promotion, and I was to do the healing procedures. My mother was one of my clients, and she said it always felt like the blood was running out of her feet. I assured her that was not happening, so she kept coming and always left feeling very relaxed.

Phyllis and I built a nice little practice together—primarily through word of mouth. Many people came in either biweekly or monthly just to relax and let their bodies heal. One man came all the way from California, as he had heard of the treatments and wanted to experience therapeutic touch while he was in Colorado. Another client always liked to look at her face before the treatment and then again after to see if her face looked any different. She claimed it did. Another client said it felt to her as if I had lifted her up and put her into the corner of the ceiling.

I went to several training sessions to learn all I could about therapeutic touch. One of the instructors said she could see blue cones of energy emitting from my chakras. She even had an artist draw a picture of me, which she hung in her therapy room. Another energy teacher I saw years later, Donna Eden, said she, too, could see blue cones of energy coming from my different chakras. I have never been able to see auras, so I just have to take their word for it.

After a couple of years, Phyllis and I decided to end our business connection, and I went on to see clients but didn't continue it as a business. Years later, I acquired a light beam generator and used it in some of the healing sessions with clients.

CHAPTER 16

RACEWALKING

During my years practicing therapeutic touch, I also took up an interest in racewalking. I had read about racewalking in several different places—enough that I began to wonder why. I've learned that when something shows up over and over, I should pay attention. So when I learned that the owner of the American Racewalk Association lived in Boulder, I checked it out. I had been going to Weight Watchers, and when I reached my goal weight, the instructor suggested we should treat ourselves to something special. She told us that her treat was to paint her house. Somehow, that didn't feel like much of a treat. I thought a lesson from the famous racewalker Viisha Sedlak would be just the ticket, so I arranged a lesson with Viisha up in Boulder. The lessons cost forty-five dollars each, which was quite a lot to spend on myself at that time.

It was winter, so the lessons were held in the field house of Colorado University. She taught me the racewalking technique—posture, arm motion, the distinct stride, but whatever you do, "don't bend your knees!" After the session was over, Viisha asked if I had noticed the man talking with her. I had. She said that he was the track coach at CU, and he had been watching me walk. He told her I was a real natural at racewalking.

I was fifty-eight years old and never felt I was a natural at anything, especially anything connected to sports. I knew I wasn't a good runner, and it's not just because I found no fun in it. Apparently, one's hips move in such a way that make the person uncomfortable when running verses racewalking. I was heavy on my feet, which is an advantage in racewalking.

I continued on with the lessons from Viisha, even received my teaching certificate from the American Racewalk Association. One of the requirements was to get a Red Cross CPR certificate. I did get it but am also happy to announce that I've never had to use it.

Viisha took a group of us to Acapulco, Mexico, for a race-walk camp. We did a 5K race on a track that had a temperature of close to 100, and the humidity reading was about the same. After the race, she asked what it was about the race that made you want to quit. Was it the heat, your legs, your breath, or your mind? None of us did quit, but all of the above applied. After the race, they had chunks of ice to sit on to cool off. Wonderful! They took videos of us that we could see later to improve our technique.

After I got my certificate, I started yet another business—this time teaching racewalking. I taught classes in Wheat

Ridge, Lakewood, and Golden. My classes included the city of Lakewood employees, cardiac ward nurses at Lutheran Hospital, the Jefferson County prison employees, adult education students, YMCA members, and many schools around Jefferson County. I even taught some nurses and doctors just before I went into surgery for my third cancer.

In 1995, I found, to my profound disappointment, that the cancer was back—this time in the left breast.

This was my third bout of this disease that kept taunting me. The second cancer struck about ten years after the first one—breast cancer in my right breast. Now it had struck again.

The doctors gave me a choice of having either a lumpectomy or a mastectomy. It was hard to make a decision. There is a no more lonely time than when you are faced with making what could be a life-and-death decision with too little information. You collect all the information you can, but when it comes right down to it, you're the only one who can make that decision.

I decided on a lumpectomy and radiation. Since it hadn't traveled outside the original site, I did not have chemotherapy. They attached drainage bottles to me, which I had to empty every so often. I wore these bottles right up until the time of the Bolder Boulder 10K Race, but I still did the race as soon as they were removed.

It looked like—and I fervently hoped—I was clear of cancer for the third time.

Racing every weekend became the norm. You could find a race-walk somewhere in the Denver area almost every weekend.

Racewalking is a judged sport that requires keeping your supporting knee straight and one foot on the ground at all times. There are always judges judging every race, and you would be disqualified if either one of these rules are broken. This allows you to move as fast as you can without running. Think of a child at the swimming pool who is instructed to "WALK, DON'T RUN!" and watch him automatically racewalk. You don't have to teach kids to racewalk—they are naturals. It's a very natural way of walking that is often made fun of and not used in everyday life.

A gentleman in one of the earlier classes I attended said he had occasion to use racewalking at the airport. He was almost late for his plane and had two briefcases with him, so he couldn't run. Walking our way allowed him to catch his plane on time.

I attended one of the master's races in Spokane, WA, but because of the recent cancer surgery, I was unable to carry my own suitcases. Several things happened in that race to let me know I was on the right track, though. There was a woman ahead of me wearing gold-colored shorts, and I happened to know she was in my same age group, so I went for the gold—shorts, that is—and passed her on a hill.

Another person said, "You are looking much better than you are feeling right now."

I always taught students to love hills—it's the best place to win a race. Once you pass someone on a hill they can hardly ever catch up to you. Another strategy is working with the wind. I knew from my flying experience that wind gives you lift if it's ahead of you or gives you a push if it's behind you. Racewalking is—as so many things are—a mental sport as well as physical.

I came home with my gold medal from that competition.

At the Senior Olympics in Baton Rouge, LA, I came home with two bronze medals, even though I was almost disqualified in one of the races for bending my knee. I didn't know I was bending it until they called me out.

Post-Bolder Boulder family photo, 1991
Left to right: Billy, Betty, Nancy, Mother

In Gillette, WY, for a qualifying race for the Senior Olympics, I met another racewalking instructor who told his students they could cheat if the judges weren't looking. I don't believe cheating is ever justified, and I couldn't help but be a little happy when none his students medaled. What a thing to teach students!

Racewalking started me on a career of walking that I have continued as I write this. But I rarely do it for competition anymore. My only competitive walk is the annual Bolder Boulder 10K Race on Memorial Day. The field of competition drops every year as I get further into my eighties, but there are still a few pretty fast old ladies out there.

CHAPTER 17

VISION QUEST

We had sold the last Dairy Queen in the spring of 1987, and I was browsing casually through the adult education catalog for the Denver metro area. I was clearly looking for a new direction in my life. By then I knew myself well enough to know I needed outside stimulation and some goals. The fear of sliding back into aimlessness and depression always lurked in the back of my mind. One offering in the catalog caught my eye: a vision quest that offered "wisdom and direction" and "spiritual guidance through transitions and challenges." *Maybe this is exactly what I am looking for!* I thought.

After reading up on it a bit more, I discovered that a vision quest is a rite of passage in some Native American cultures. During a quest, the "seeker"—in this case, me—heads out into the wilderness for three days for the purpose of seeing a vision, revealing their purpose through isolation, fasting, prayer, and meditation. The objective is for one to make a connection to the spirits that will help them find their purpose in life, their role in a community, and how they may best serve.

I signed up. Harold supported me and understood it was something I had to do on my own, so he agreed to hold down the fort at home.

The get-acquainted presentation took place in Lakewood, where we were introduced to the leader, Leav Bolender. When Leav and I actually talked over the stalls in the ladies' room, I decided this was someone I could trust to take me to a place I didn't know and camp for three days and nights by myself.

The idea was to be totally alone, with no reading material and no food, for three days—get to really know yourself and what you are about. We were to take an item with us that reminded us of something we no longer wanted in our lives. One brought her divorce papers; another had letters from her father that said he no longer wanted her in his life. Everything was to be thrown into a bonfire to rid ourselves of burdens we had carried. For weeks prior to leaving, I recorded onto a cassette tape all the things I no longer wanted in my life: the times I felt I had been a victim. I no longer wanted victimhood to rule my life. All these things made for a large, hot fire, accompanied by many tears.

Before the trip began, I learned to fast for three days and carry a heavy backpack on fairly long walks. I felt as prepared as I could be—that is, if you can prepare for an experience that you can't prepare for.

While there were twenty-two "seekers" meeting at the base-camp outside Moab, UT, four of us were coming from the

Denver area. So the four of us new friends drove the seven-hour trip together in my van. Although we didn't know each other when we met at 8:00 a.m. and left the Front Range, we sure did by 3:00 p.m. when we arrived at our meeting place in the middle of Nowhere, UT.

Our first night at camp, we met everyone and Leav taught us how to set up our tarps. Then she left us to practice on our own. I was immediately lost. I had no clue how to do this. Things got even more difficult when it started to rain. I struggled with setting up the tarp, and with the rain pummeling down, I finally gave up and went back to sleep in our van.

The next morning we formed a circle and Leav went around and asked how we had done our first night. I mentioned I had trouble setting up, and she asked me, "Who did you ask for help?"

That was my first lesson: to recognize how reluctant I am to ask for help when it is available and I'm with people who are more than happy to help. One fellow asked if it bothered me to go sleep in the van. I told him it would have been pretty stupid to have a warm, dry car handy and not sleep in it while it poured and I couldn't figure out how to set up my camp.

After our debrief about the first night, we started out on our personal journeys. We were assigned a partner with whom we would start out down the same trail, then a few miles into our hiking, we were instructed to find separate spots to claim as our own and not see each other again for the three days. My partner was Julie. After we claimed our respective spots, we needed to find an agreed upon spot where we would leave notes to let the other know we were okay—she in the morning and me in the evening.

We had hiked about two miles down the trail when I found the perfect place for my camp. It had two large flat rocks with a few bushes around, the mountains in the background and a small stream I could use for drinking water after adding iodine to it. We all had to add iodine to prevent giardia, the intestinal parasite you get from unpurified water. I could hardly drink the water with the taste of iodine by the time camp was over.

On the first night in my spot, I struggled with that darn tarp again. I wrestled and jerry-rigged it enough that it suited its purpose of keeping me protected from the elements. Thank God it wasn't a tarp beauty contest!

In the middle of the night I desperately needed to pee, but I didn't dare get up and leave the safety of my tarp. I imagined all the wild animals right outside my tarp, just waiting for me to have to pee, then they would pounce on me and eat me for a snack. I held it in.

I finally couldn't hold it anymore. I crawled out, looked both ways—as if I could see anything in the darkest of the dark—felt my way around by foot, did my business, and threw myself back into the tarp in record time. Of course it was uneventful. No one was standing outside my tarp ready to murder me, and no animal was ready to gut me and have me for lunch. Everything was fine. Even pleasant.

There was the second big lesson of my vision quest: that all my fears are stories my imagination has conjured up. Fears are not based in reality. In fact, some say FEAR stands for False Evidence Appearing Real.

On the second day, I took some short day hikes around the area, but I never stayed away from my little camp for very long.

On one of my short hikes, I found a great big rock and climbed up to take a seat. From the rock I looked around and noted the scenery, I watched lizards doing push-ups and felt a slight wind, when all of a sudden these words became so strong in my body: "Shut that damn kid up; she's getting on my nerves."

My back went straight up sitting on that rock, and I heard it again, "Shut that damn kid up; she's getting on my nerves."

What did it mean?! Where did it come from?! It wasn't just the words, it was the feeling; a dense, harsh, painful feeling that swept through me: "Shut that damn kid up; she's getting on my nerves." I cried and cried for a very long time on top of that rock.

Much later, when I mentioned this to my brother, he said, "That would have been Dad."

I believe he was right. It made me wonder just how old I was when I heard this and how it had affected the rest of my life.

The third night out, we were told to stay awake all night and ask for our Indian name. I gathered twigs and small sticks to keep a little fire going so I could stay awake. I had been aware that the constellation Orion would be coming up just before dawn and eagerly awaited its appearance. I thought it was pretty silly to ask for an Indian name and was not surprised when I didn't get one. But wouldn't it have been great to be something like Strong Bear or Running Deer? Nothing showed up, however, and the night was finally over.

Many weeks later, long after I arrived back home, I sat straight up in bed one morning and knew my Indian name. I had no memory of a dream or why I knew it was my name, but I just knew it was my name: Flame Woman.

Months later, I had occasion to hear a Native American chief speak at a program in Boulder. He spoke of his vision of a mountain where everyone lived together happily. The mountain was spewing flames and represented the oneness of everyone living in peace. The name Flame Woman took on a whole new meaning.

After spending three nights on our own in the desert, we all hiked out of our respective spots and gathered to discuss our experiences. Some shared about their fears that never actually happened. No one got lost; people shed tears and survived the fasting. One woman was scared to death of seeing scorpions, and she was the only one who saw scorpions.

We shared stories, giggled, cried, and ate. Oh, we ate. Leav came loaded with food for twenty-two people. Pots and pans over the fire boiling pasta by the bushel, and fruit being passed around and around.

In the beginning, Leav told us that no matter what happens you can't do a vision quest wrong. She said it would affect everything that happened in our lives from that point onward. She was right on both counts. We were twenty-two people having a shared experience alone.

After the quest, I was invited to speak to different groups about my experience. Interestingly, most people wanted to know about the weather. Admittedly, it was difficult to know just how much it had really affected me.

The following year, one of my new friends, Pam, and I were asked to co-lead the group, so we stayed in base camp while the new group went out. We even made a quick trip back into Moab to a T-shirt shop and also to do the thing I had wanted to do more than anything else while I was on my vision quest—to sit on a real toilet.

As I'd prepared for my vision quest, I went out for walks every morning. It was Harold's and my custom to walk from our home in Lakewood to Crown Hill Lake, which was just over a mile from our house along 26th Avenue. Some mornings, Harold would not go with me, but I had no qualms about going by myself.

This particular morning, it was quite dark. As I walked up the hill a couple of blocks from our home, the words, "Turn back Dick Whittington, Lord Mayor of London," came into my head for no apparent reason. The saying was from a story about a mayor of London, written about the 1300s mayor and his cat. He had been leaving town, and the church bells rang out the words. Why would that pop into my head? But I kept walking. Again, the words, "Turn back Dick Whittington, Lord Mayor of London." The third time it happened, I still didn't understand but thought I'd better listen. I turned around and went back home.

Early the next morning, we heard the screams of a woman nearby but didn't know what it was about or where it came from. Later that morning, Harold and I both went out and noticed a police car sitting in almost the exact spot where I had turned back. The policeman came over to us and asked if we walked there often. We said we did, and then he told us the story of what had happened the day before.

A woman walking up the hill had been kidnapped there and taken to the mountains, raped, badly beaten, and left severely injured. He felt that the kidnapper had been lying in wait for a woman to come by—possibly for days.

He probably was there when I turned back, but I was not aware of him. If there is a lesson in that, it might be this: don't question so much what comes into your knowing. Just listen. I'm glad I chose to listen that time.

CHAPTER 18

BIKING

In August of 1998, when we were sixty-seven and sixty-eight years old respectively, Harold and I took up biking. We hadn't biked before but saw an Elder Hostel program about a guided trip from Deggendorf, Germany, to Vienna, Australia, and what better way to start a new hobby than to dive in with an eight-day, 250-mile bike ride in Europe?

Our neighbors Russ and Betsy Krueger decided to join us. We practiced riding some distances before we left, and when we got to Germany we had a half day of instructions to learn the rules of the road from Frank, our leader. Frank had very definite ideas of how a guided ride should be structured—leave quite a lot of space between riders, never pass the leader, and the sweep passes no one (the sweep is a rider at the very end who makes sure no one gets left behind). At each corner, he planted one of the riders to indicate the direction the rest of the group was to take, thereby making sure everyone knew which way to go, even if there was a lot of space between. When the sweep showed up, the corner person could leave, and Frank would appoint someone else for the next corner. He chose a new sweep every day, but Frank was always the leader. His system worked.

Before we started each morning, someone from the area came to speak to us. It was usually someone from the area who would talk about the crafts and history of that region. The unification of Germany, which was happening at that time, was also a hot topic of interest.

On the morning of our fiftieth wedding anniversary, September 4, two of our fellow riders picked us a bouquet of wildflowers to tie onto our handlebars. That evening in Grein, Austria, Frank and the crew got us the honeymoon suite. After dinner, Frank called a meeting in a room on the second floor. He didn't tell us what the meeting was about, but upon arriving, Frank was playing his guitar and the whole gang erupted into a singalong. One of the riders recited a poem to us in both German and English. Our singalong was interrupted when the lights went out, the door opened, and the owner of the hotel carried in a huge torte with fifty candles and champagne. What a wonderful party we had—and all totally unexpected! A beautiful way to celebrate our fifty years together.

After we came home, Harold and I set up a riding group using Frank's model. It really helps to keep track of everybody, and it helps ensure their safety and fun.

In 2003, we led our first out-of-town bike ride. We gathered eight couples and prepared to ride the 225 miles along the Katy Trail from Clinton to St. Charles, almost to St. Louis.

The Katy Trail is a "rails to trails" route, part of the collection of old railroad lines that have been converted into very walkable and ridable trails. For a group our age, ranging from sixty to eighty, we prefer the "rails to trails." They keep us off the roads and away from traffic for a more relaxing ride. Those old railroad routes are remarkably scenic and beautiful.

About half the trail follows the Missouri River—a beautiful ride! We chose the fall of the year, hoping it would be a little cooler and the fall colors would be at their peak. They did not let us down. We saw several stations where Lewis and Clark had stopped along their route.

The condition of the trail spoiled us for some other trails we have ridden: it was hard-packed, crushed limestone, and mostly level. As in Germany, we had one really rainy day, but we just kept riding and "singing in the rain."

Since Harold and I were leaders that first day, I explained to the group after the ride that I would like to be referred to as "Queen of the Universe" because I had such a responsible job that day. Dick responded, "You sound more like Colonel Klink to me." But to this day, Dick refers to me as Queen of the Universe.

We continued these fall rides for about ten years. After the Katy, we rode the Mickelson Trail through the Black Hills of South Dakota. We rode in Iowa, Illinois, Idaho, Minnesota, Wisconsin, Michigan, Nebraska, Wyoming, from Pittsburgh to Washington, DC, and the Mickelson and the Katy twice. The

Pittsburgh to Washington trip ended with a tour of the White House arranged by one of our government employed riders who was staying on to do some work in the White House.

Around the County Custer County Chronicle • June 23, 2004 • Page 11

Betty and Harold at the end of the 114-mile Mickelson Trail, South Dakota, 2004

Several local newspapers sent reporters to interview us, apparently because we were such a lot of "not young" riders from out of state wearing matching T-shirts.

One of the younger riders who passed us told his friend, "It looks like Hell's Angels to me."

Over the years other people have joined our group. As long as they were willing to abide by our rules, they were welcome. Our biking friends have been a big part of our lives.

Our last overseas ride was a bike and barge in Provence, France. For me, this trip wasn't as fun as some of the others, although we saw a lot of interesting beautiful countryside. There were too many big trucks driving too fast along narrow roads for my liking. Once I got lost when I went straight ahead instead of turning when I should have. But the leader found me, and everything turned out well.

Over the next few years, our biking friends slowly stopped biking altogether—balance issues were the main culprit. Those issues took a toll on our group, but we still get together and eat when possible—our second most favorite activity. Ed, our oldest and usually the fastest, often said we were more of a talking and eating group than a riding group. So, although we're still very close, the biking trips came to a natural end.

CHAPTER 19

GOLDEN YEARS

Harold and I sold our Lakewood house in 1994 and moved to a perfect patio home on the edge of Golden's New Loveland Mine Park. It had the two-car garage that made Harold happy and a pantry that made me happy. When we eventually put in a heated bathroom floor and a walk-in tub with twenty air-jets, I wanted for nothing.

Golden become our home like none of the others over the years. Due to the walks we lead every Wednesday morning, we got to know all the business owners, the government workers, and the Chamber of Commerce employees. The Mayor of Golden actually honored Harold and me with a Mayor's Award in 2016 for "serving as inspiring role models and ambassadors for healthy living and walking in Golden."

Congressional Record

United States of America
PROCEEDINGS AND DEBATES OF THE 114th CONGRESS, FIRST SESSION

House of Representatives

Mr. Speaker, I rise today to recognize and applaud Betty & Harold Payte for receiving the Golden Mayor's Award for Excellence.

Betty and Harold Payte are role models and community activists for healthy living. Both in their mid-eighties, they are thoughtful, caring, and inclusive leaders who have attracted a large and loyal following to their weekly community "walk and talks" through Golden. In all weather and all seasons, for people of all ages and abilities, with residents from all over the metropolitan area, the Paytes share their joy in moving through Golden's beautiful outdoor environment. Betty roams up and down the line of walkers to make sure everyone has a walking partner and to see if anyone needs extra encouragement. Harold, a humorous storyteller, usually serves as "sweep" at the back of the group with slower-paced walkers; the Paytes encourage all of us to live full, joyful, healthy lives.

I congratulate Betty & Harold Payte for being the recipient of this well-deserved honor by Mayor Marjorie Sloan, and I thank them for their continued commitment to the people and families they serve.

Thank you,

Ed Perlmutter
Member of Congress

Betty and Harold's Golden Mayor's Award for Excellence, 2016

When we moved to Golden, I noticed the signs saying it was just over twenty miles between Golden and Boulder. Something about that was a challenge, and in the back of my mind, I thought, "Someday, I would like to walk that trip."

Three years ago, it felt like it was the time. It didn't matter to me whether I walked it by myself or had others join me. As it turned out, there were about eight of us, and our friends Jack and Peg drove sag wagon and followed along. My plan was to do it on Father's Day, a Sunday, when the traffic would be lighter and the weather wouldn't be too hot. Wrong on all counts. We had really heavy traffic all the way on a fairly narrow road, and the temperature rose to over 100 degrees. Four of the people had planned to walk only a segment and dropped out after about five miles. Harold, Mike, Dawn, and I continued down the road. Jack and Peg continued to stop every now and then to replenish our water supply.

Dawn and I walked most of the time together. We stopped at the bus stop about a third of the way, where there was a little shelter house. We sat and took off our shoes for a while. Ahh, such relief! Strangely, while we were walking, we didn't do much talking. Most of the time, there was too much noise from the traffic in close proximity to us. And even when there wasn't traffic, we enjoyed the reprieve and quiet so much that we didn't talk.

Another one of our walkers was Mike L. He is mostly blind and cannot hear well but is very strong and determined. He took the last bus out of Denver the night before and slept in the park overnight, so he could be there at five o'clock in the morning to do the walk with us. At one point, Mike and I were walking together, and I thought, *Here we are, an almost blind and deaf man, and an eighty-five-year-old woman, with temperatures over 100 degrees on a narrow, busy road—people probably think we're crazy.* And they were probably right.

Just as we topped the last long hill and could see Boulder in the distance, it was a most beautiful sight. The Boulder Flatirons formed a backdrop with a great green valley stretching out below us. It took our breath away. I immediately started crying and the lyrics, "No, no, they can't take that away from me," started to play over and over in my head.

When we were within a few miles of downtown Boulder, Harold and I started to show signs of heat stroke. We both insisted we were fine and just needed a bit of rest in the shade, but Peg got nervous and called the medics to check us out. The medics soared up the highway in record time, complete with sirens and swirling lights. They checked us out and were worried, but more so about their realization that we had been walking on this busy road in 100-degree heat than our current health. They were impressed. While we sat in the ambulance cooling down and getting hydrated, Amy and Jim came to check on us and were just shy of insisting that we finish another time. Almost any other time that wasn't the hottest day of the year!

It was a bit crushing to not finish our walk from Golden to Boulder that day, but we noted exactly where we finished and immediately made a plan to come back on another day to that same spot and finish off the final miles. Since our anniversary is September 4, we would make that an extra special occasion by completing our Golden to Boulder trip.

In the meantime, the whole gang piled into the cars and went to Amy and Jim's, where Jim made refreshing, rejuvenating drinks for everyone. No matter that we didn't get to the finish line—we had accomplished much more than we'd bargained for: walking in significant traffic on a very narrow pathway in the midst of extreme heat. There was much to celebrate.

Betty and Harold doing what they do best:
leading a walk in Golden, Colorado

There is a local walking group called Walk2Connect. It's a co-op group that offers guided walks—both short and long—all over Colorado, but primarily in the Denver metro area. They even teach people to be guides and urge them to put together their own guided walks. Some walks are tougher hikes through the Colorado mountain trails, and others are shorter walks through neighborhoods in the city. Some—our favorites—include food!

Harold and I got connected with Walk2Connect through Saoirse, a city councilwoman in Golden. She had heard of me and invited Harold and me to lead a group of walkers in Golden. Teaching racewalking was not what it was about. It was simply intended to lead a group on short walks around town. To date, our group regularly hosts twenty to thirty people every Wednesday morning. Most of the walks end up being a little more about talking than walking. All are welcome. We've even had three-year-olds with grandparents and an assortment of dogs that really love being together for a leisurely walk. These walking groups have gone well beyond the weekly gathering and have formed great friendships.

One of our favorite Walk2Connect walks is called the Sunday Morning Mosey. We meet every Sunday morning, rain or shine, at a local restaurant, walk five-ish miles, and return to the restaurant to eat and have some laughs.

Every Sunday morning as we would assemble, I noticed a man sitting at a booth by himself. I'm not sure why, but I went over and asked him to join us. He didn't look very much like a walker, with his tank top, arms covered with tattoos, long hair, and beard almost completely covering his face. His response was to look at me like I was crazy even to ask, and he said no.

Every week he sat in the same place, and every week I went over and asked if he was ready to join us.

"No, I work all week standing on my feet. Why would I want to walk on Sundays?"

"It's too hot."

"It's too cold," he growled at me.

After many months, he started to smile at me when I walked in. Then I learned that his name was Scott, and soon he was showing me pictures of his grandkids and telling me the history of his tattoos. I kept asking if he wanted to join us, and he kept saying no.

One day he said, "No, I'm not going to walk with you today, but don't stop asking."

On the following New Year's Day, we gathered for our

usual Sunday Morning Mosey, when we noticed that Scott's booth was empty. The waitress, in a teary voice, told us he had unexpectedly died in his sleep the night before. It was a shock but a great lesson for me: "JUST BECAUSE SOMEONE SAYS NO, DON'T STOP ASKING."

CHAPTER 20

GEOCACHING

Three years before our bike ride in France, Harold and I started another new hobby—geocaching. Geocaching is a GPS-based hide-and-seek treasure hunt. Small, waterproof containers (caches) are strategically hidden all over the world in sneaky, cheeky locations. There are clues to find them. I read recently that there have been more than a million caches hidden. Each cache contains a logbook for discoverers to sign. People often add little trinkets to the container for the next person to find. People of all ages like geocaching—from children to, well, Harold and me.

While on our bike ride in Provence, most of the riders spent long lunch hours at the outdoor tables drinking and enjoying the local wines. We went geocaching. We met a young couple from Germany who were also looking, and while we didn't speak the same language, we were able to communicate through the international language of geocaching. We found a cache on the outside of an old cathedral together.

To date, we have found over 1,500 caches. On a local level, one time, we found a cache that wanted us to add a limerick when we logged in our find. We came up with this little ditty ...

There once was a couple from Golden
Who didn't think they were too olden
To go geocaching ... in fact ... found it smashing
Instead of just sitting home moldin'.

THAT DARN CANCER

IS BACK

Cancer reared its ugly head again in 2018—just when I thought I'd whipped it for good—eighteen years after the last cancer in my right breast.

It started with an excruciating headache that landed me in Lutheran Hospital. I very seldom get headaches, and this one was unbearable. The next morning, they took an X-ray that showed there was a small cancer eating away at my skull.

The doctors soon set me up with an MRI of my head and a PET scan of my entire body. They said then that the cancer had originated in the left breast and traveled to my skull and my left hip and thigh. The lesion in the skull was too deep for a biopsy or surgery, so they decided to start radiation right away. They scheduled me for ten treatments on my skull and left leg, starting immediately. The treatments on my head were as uncomfortable as you can imagine, as they had to clamp my head into a vise. No pain involved, just my head clamped into a vise.

The disappointment of finding cancer again was soul crushing. Fourteen years earlier, our friends Ross and Betsy Krueger had loaned me a book by medical researcher Colin Campbell—*The China Study*. Ross had been a research scientist, and Betsy had also worked in research. *The China Study* made a compelling argument for changing your diet to a vegan or plant-based diet to ward off cancer and other diseases. I chose to go for it and changed my diet immediately to a plant-based diet. Harold said he wanted to support me, so he'd give it a shot for a few weeks. We've both followed it religiously for fourteen years to date.

So when I found out the cancer was back, the disappointment was profound. But I consoled myself that at least it had been eighteen years since the last one. And a stunningly healthy and active eighteen years it's been.

After the second cancer in 1980, I asked the doctor if there was anything I could do to keep it from coming back, and his answer was, "Eat anything you want; you deserve it." Did he not know any better? Or did he assume I was going to die anyhow, so it didn't matter what I ate? I have always appreciated what the doctors have done to help me, but I have always thought it was up to me to do anything I can to help myself. I may not always be right but I'm willing to check around and see what I can do.

We actually enjoy the vegan way of eating and have no problem staying on course. But when this cancer started, I thought maybe a piece of salmon would be good. I got one small helping down, but the next time I tried it, I could not swallow it. So cancer or not, vegan is still the way we eat.

Right now, a year and a half later, I am feeling well, and the cancer has stopped. My balance isn't as good as I would like, but I feel it is constantly improving. I was in the locker room at the community center one morning, and several women were standing around talking about their balance problems. One of the older ladies who was changing into her swimsuit said, "When you get to be ninety, your balance sure doesn't improve." I asked if she was over ninety. She said yes. I said, "I wouldn't know, I'm only eighty-seven." She slapped the back of her hand to her forehead and wailed, "Oh, to be eighty-seven again!"

One night after I had been in for a treatment, I felt terrible. My head hurt, and I was dizzy and nauseous. I was sitting on the couch with my head in my hands, too dizzy to walk, feeling too sick and disheartened to do anything but sit there.

Suddenly, I remembered a conversation I'd had with Amy, the waitress at Caitlin's Restaurant where we meet every Sunday morning for our five-mile Mosey. She was telling us her husband was quite ill and on dialysis. They were looking for a kidney transplant. Into my mind came the knowledge that all things are possible, and I told her that. As I was sitting on the sofa, all of a sudden, that statement came back to me, and I saw clearly that I must get well so that her husband Gaylenn knew he could. All my symptoms immediately disappeared, and I stood up and went in to wash the dishes. All things are possible, and we have the responsibility to accept them.

Gaylenn has since had his operation—with wife, Amy, being a perfect kidney match—and they are both doing well. Truly, all things are possible.

CHAPTER 22

AWAKENING DAY
APRIL 9, 2019

Mark I awaken to the light of my own true nature.

I had been dealing with this latest version of cancer for over a year. It was on my mind all the time, and suddenly, on awakening, came the statement, "Let go and let God." It seemed the most natural thing in the world to do.

The rest of my day went like this: I started by going to the sauna to clean out old, hung-onto toxins, then on to the chiropractor for a treatment. He said he thought my body was doing a lot better. I was expecting a call later from Dr. Kosler, the oncologist, so I hoped that this was a sign of good news. Dr. Scott, my chiropractor, said to try to keep a positive attitude about the call.

For the previous two weeks, I had undergone tests of various kinds: a head MRI, a PET scan, and many blood tests. Normally, I would have been very worried about the news I was about to hear, but since my early morning notice, nothing seemed to bother me too much.

I decided that Harold and I should go out and search for some geocaches, which is something we hadn't done in over a year. It would help keep me relaxed while I waited to get The Call. The first geocache we looked for was supposed to be in a rock pile at the top of a very steep ravine. Just after we pulled up, two different cars stopped to see if we had a problem—wonderful, caring people. Harold did find the cache, and we went on to find another, then on to look for one that showed on the map as being on the top of Green Mountain. I had not tried anything nearly that difficult in well over a year, and the trail was quite steep, narrow, and rocky; it was quite intimidating.

While we didn't make it quite all the way to the top, we were just slightly below it when we turned around so Harold could look for the cache, which appeared to be just off the trail. I did not want him to go off-trail by himself, as it was steep and scary looking. He did it anyway. I thought at the time, "This is my last geocaching trip because this is not fun." As I watched from above, I saw someone, who looked to be a ranger, on the trail below. Sure enough, Harold turned around and came back after the ranger told him he was not to be off trail at any time.

We headed back down, meeting the ranger again, who apologized for spoiling our trip. I explained I was grateful because I didn't want Harold to do that anyway. We had a nice chat with him about geocaching and the possibility of him trying it with his son—a very nice guy.

On the way up, a tall, pretty blond passed us—which wasn't too hard to do—and went all the way to the top. We met her on the way down … her hair was blowing out behind her, and a story, "The Tortoise and the Hare," came to mind. We were definitely "the tortoise," and she was "the hair." She laughed when I told her.

Another young woman stopped to chat with us and told us about her eighty-three-year-old mother's passing about two weeks before. She went on down the trail, then turned around and came back to take our picture. When we got to the bottom, the ranger was busy bandaging up a biker who had fallen on the trail and was pretty scratched up.

It was time to go home. To face the inevitable phone call. Then she called.

I took a deep breath as I answered the phone. Then exhaled when she told me there was no change for the worse, and I was to keep on doing what I was doing and come back in three months.

I felt great relief, but I was so ready for anything—whether that be "good" or "bad." Yet, I couldn't help but think that the whole day had been like some kind of verification that "all is well."

As I reflected on this latest bit of news, on my life thus far, and on the continued journey ahead, those words played over and over in my head. Through a bout of mental illness, four experiences with cancer, and facing the scary, the new, as well as the unknown, I am certain that whatever the future brings, ALL WILL INDEED BE WELL.

Harold and Betty living a full life

LETTER TO MY GRANDCHILDREN

Dear Grandchildren, Great-Grandchildren, and Future
Generations,

I've experienced a lot since I was that ten-year-old I addressed
so many years ago. I hope these pages have captured some of
what I learned about myself over the years. All those little events
were insignificant at the time. But string them together and they
make up the arc of my life—and part of your history.

Perhaps the biggest overall lesson I have learned is: LISTEN
to your inner guidance.

I've also learned: Summon up the COURAGE and
STRENGTH to go through the tough times you may be faced
with.

Have the CURIOSITY to learn to do things you know nothing about but want to learn.

Find the PERSISTENCE to see things through, never giving
in to procrastination.

Above all else, never, never give up.

An old saying that has served me well states, "Into every life a little rain must fall sounds like a dire prediction, but every life needs a little rain for the flowers to bloom." May that habit of looking on the bright side serve you well.

One of the most important things I have realized is just how many loving, caring, and helpful relatives, friends, and professional people surrounded me in my travels.

And so, I say to you, as I said to my ten-year-old self:

Go into whatever is next with your eyes wide open, head held high, standing tall. Trust yourself, embrace the silly, the tough, and the annoying. Remember to have fun, and according to Glen's 103-year-old mother, "Never miss a chance for a bite of chocolate."

Always remember, you were meant to be here. Don't take life too seriously. Discover the joy in your lives. Look for it.

BLOOM ON!

Eighty-eight and counting,
Still and always,
Betty

Acknowledgments

A constant blessing through my life has been the endless parade of supportive people at every turn.

To my parents, Bill and Winnie Klein, for making me tough enough to face whatever was thrown at me. I feel they did the best they knew how.

My endless gratitude to my late brother, Bill, who first suggested I should write my life story back in the '90s, and to my sister, Nancy, for sharing life's journey.

To our daughters, Patty and Amy, who must have wondered at times, "What in the world is going on?"

It takes a lot of people with various skill sets to put together a condensed life story that spans eighty-eight years. I would like to acknowledge some of them here. To Rosemary Rawson who helped pull out some of the precious details from the past eight decades. I enjoyed our weekly -- sometimes nightly -- phone calls, and the discovery of our many similar experiences. I could live another eighty-eight years and not thank you enough.

To Polly Letofsky of My Word Publishing – and, ahem, "leader" of our Sunday morning Mosey, without her help and prodding this would have never been scribbled down on paper.

To the editorial staff, Bobby Haas, Donna Mazzitelli, and Jen Zelinger, who helped to poke and fuss and rearrange to get these first eighty-eight years together in some sort of readable form.

And as always, to my greatest support, Harold, for holding my hand from that first date on the train, and still seventy-one years later. Sometimes we had to lean into each other just to get through, but lean we did.

Made in the USA
Las Vegas, NV
11 November 2023

80649398R00083